Trade Blocs

A World Bank Policy Research Report

Trade Blocs

Published for the World Bank
OXFORD UNIVERSITY PRESS

Oxford University Press

OXFORD   NEW YORK   ATHENS   AUCKLAND   BANGKOK   BOGOTA   BUENOS AIRES
CALCUTTA   CAPE TOWN   CHENNAI   DAR ES SALAAM   DELHI   FLORENCE   HONG
KONG   ISTANBUL   KARACHI   KUALA LUMPUR   MADRID   MELBOURNE   MEXICO CITY
MUMBAI   NAIROBI   PARIS   SÃO PAULO   SINGAPORE   TAIPEI   TOKYO   TORONTO
WARSAW

and associated companies in

BERLIN   IBADAN

© *2000 The International Bank for Reconstruction*
and Development / The World Bank
1818 H Street, N.W., Washington, D.C. 20433, USA

Published by Oxford University Press, Inc.
198 Madison Avenue, New York, N.Y. 10016

Manufactured in the United States of America
First printing August 2000

The findings, interpretations, and conclusions expressed in this study are entirely those of
the authors and should not be attributed in any manner to the World Bank, to its affiliated
organizations, or to members of its Board of Executive Directors or the countries they
represent. The boundaries, colors, denominations, and other information shown on any
map in this volume do not imply on the part of the World Bank Group any judgment on
the legal status of any territory or the endorsement or acceptance of such boundaries.

Library of Congress Cataloging-in-Publication Number: 00-028297

Contents

Tables

Foreword

THERE HAS BEEN A VERITABLE EXPLOSION OF REGIONAL integration agreements (RIAs) in the last 15 years or so. Nearly every country in the world is either a member of—or discussing participation in—one or more regional integration arrangements. Such agreements have been concluded among high-income countries, among low-income countries, and, more recently, starting with the North American Free Trade Area (NAFTA)—between high-income and developing countries. More than half of world trade now occurs within actual or prospective trading blocs. Why are countries so active in their pursuit of preferential trade agreements? Do such agreements allow countries to obtain benefits that cannot be achieved through autonomous actions or multilateral cooperation? Or is it an instance of "old wine in new bottles," as argued by opponents of regional arrangements who regard them as the outcome of political economy forces fostering discriminatory trade restrictions and undermining the multilateral trading system?

Although regional integration has given rise to a vigorous debate—one that shows few signs of dying down—the quality of interchange is frequently low. There is often a lack of understanding of what determines the economic effects of a RIA and ignorance of the available evidence on the various potential justifications that are offered for pursuing RIAs. Few of the more recent arguments in favor of RIAs have been satisfactorily formalized or tested—for example, that regionalism stimulates investment, that it confers credibility on reform programs, or that it assists multilateral liberalization—and no attempt has been made to weigh them against each other in the circumstances of developing countries. At the same time, economists in particular have not paid enough attention to the noneconomic objectives that frequently underlie RIAs, and the role of trade preferences in achieving these objectives. Understanding the potential linkages between favoritism in trade and the pursuit of noneconomic political and social objectives is crucial in deciding both the bottom line question of whether to join a RIA, and the negotiation question of what design is most suitable.

This report summarizes the findings of a research project to understand better the political economy of regional integration, the economic benefits and costs for developing countries, the policy choices confronting governments, and the implications of regionalism for nonmembers and the multilateral trading system.

Regional agreements frequently have political objectives and noneconomic dimensions, including national security, enhancement of bargaining power, and bolstering the credibility of reforms (economic and political). The report concludes that attainment of such political objectives depends primarily on agreement design, as this determines the size and distribution of net economic impacts. Economic gains depend on securing an effective increase in competition on the regional market and minimizing incentives for consumers to start purchasing goods and services from inefficient regional suppliers. This can be achieved by increasing openness to trade with the outside world at the same time as intraregional trade is being liberalized. One central finding of the report is that selecting high-income countries as partners is often likely to be the best option for developing countries. Industrial countries tend to have lower barriers, there is greater scope for exploitation of comparative advantage, and a higher probability of attaining political objectives. Agreements among developing countries are more likely to lead to income divergence of members, causing potential for implementation problems and tensions.

Deeper and wider forms of integration may be required to realize sought-after benefits of greater competition and economies of scale in production. These forms of integration include agreements that go beyond abolition of tariffs to include other (national) policies that affect trade in goods, such as customs procedures, product conformity assessment requirements, abolition of antidumping and safeguard protection, as well as investment and services policies. Such forms of integration often can and should be applied on a nondiscriminatory basis, in which case regional agreements will complement the multilateral trading system. But experience to date suggests that achieving deeper and wider integration is not easy. Few extant agreements involving developing countries have gone significantly beyond the preferential reduction of border barriers. Deeper forms of integration frequently will require the creation of mechanisms to ensure an equitable distribution of gains.

Making regional integration an effective element of national development strategies is a great challenge. Regional agreements can reduce the frictional costs of trade by harmonizing regulations and standards. By making national policies a part of international agreements, regional agreements can increase the credibility of reform initiatives and strengthen security arrangements between partners. They can be vehicles for governments to test the waters of freer trade. By reducing trade barriers on a subset of partners, however, countries generally increase the real cost of their imports, reduce the flow of technology from nonmember countries, and increase dependence on particular export markets. Great care is required to ensure that such costs are compensated by other gains. If not, membership may hinder, rather than promote, development.

Like previous Policy Research Reports, this study is the product of the staff of the World Bank: the judgments and arguments made herein do not necessarily reflect the views of the World Bank's Board of Directors or the governments they represent.

Josef Ritzen
Vice President, Development Policy
The World Bank

Acknowledgments

THE PROJECT HAS BENEFITED GREATLY FROM THE WORK OF the many scholars who prepared background papers. Bernard Hoekman and Peter Robson contributed to early drafts of the report. Jaime De Melo and Simon Everett provided useful comments. Excellent research assistance was provided by Soamiely Andriamananjara, Won Chang, Anju Gupta, Moonhui Kim, Praveen Kumar, and Isidro Soloaga. Lawrence MacDonald and Joost Polak provided valuable editorial services. Mary-Ann Arouna, Maria Lourdes Kasilag, and Rebecca Martin provided superb administrative support throughout the duration of the project.

The Research Project and Team

T HE PRINCIPAL AUTHORS OF THIS POLICY RESEARCH REPORT were Paul Collier, Maurice Schiff, Anthony Venables, and L. Alan Winters. The report draws on the findings of a large research project on regional integration led by Maurice Schiff and L. Alan Winters, who—with Bernard Hoekman—prepared the first draft of the report. The magnitude of the research output generated by the project is too large to do full justice in this report. A more detailed, book-length analysis and assessment of regional integration that draws in greater depth on the results of the research project is being prepared by Maurice Schiff, L. Alan Winters, and Bernard Hoekman. Interested readers can download many of the background papers from the World Bank trade website at www.worldbank.org/trade. A number of papers were published in a special issue of the *World Bank Economic Review* (May 1998).

CHAPTER 1

Regional Integration Agreements

Introduction

THE GROWTH OF REGIONAL TRADING BLOCS—OFTEN KNOWN as regional integration agreements (RIAs)—is one of the major international relations developments of recent years. Most industrial and developing countries in the world are members of a regional integration agreement, and many belong to more than one: more than one-third of world trade takes place within such agreements.[1] The structure of regional agreements varies hugely, but all have one thing in common—the objective of reducing barriers to trade between member countries. At their simplest they merely remove tariffs on intrabloc trade in goods, but many go beyond that to cover nontariff barriers and to extend liberalization to trade and investment. At their deepest they have the objective of economic union, and they involve the construction of shared executive, judicial, and legislative institutions.

During the last decade the move to regionalism has become a headlong rush. Figure 1.1 gives the number of regional agreements notified to the General Agreement on Trade and Tariffs and the World Trade Organization (GATT/WTO)[2] each year, and makes apparent the dramatic increase that occurred in the 1990s. Of the 194 agreements notified at the beginning of 1999, 87 were notified since 1990. Description of some of the major agreements made in recent years is given in box 1.1, and table 1.1 lists selected trading blocs, their memberships—and their acronyms.

The last 10 years have witnessed qualitative, as well as quantitative, changes in regional integration schemes. There have been three major developments.

The first is the recognition that effective integration requires more than reducing tariffs and quotas. Many other barriers have the effect of segmenting markets and impeding the free flow of goods, services, investments, and

1

Figure 1.1 Notifications to GATT and WTO of Regional Integration Agreements, 1949–98

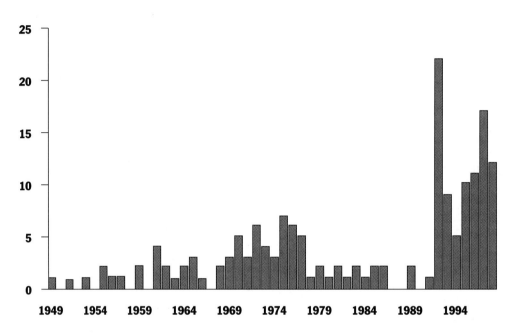

Notifications

Source: WTO data.

ideas, and wide ranging policy measures—going well beyond traditional trade policies—are needed to remove these barriers. This so-called deep integration was first actively pursed in the Single Market Program of the European Union (EU), and elements of this program are now finding their way into the debate in other regional agreements.

The second is the move from "closed regionalism" to a more open model. Many of the trading blocs that were formed between developing countries in the 1960s and 1970s were based on a model of import-substituting development, and regional agreements—with high external trade barriers—were used as a way of implementing this model.[3] The new wave of regional agreements—including resurrection of some old agreements—have generally been more outward-looking, and more committed to boosting, rather than controlling, international commerce.

The third development is the advent of trade blocs in which both high-income industrial countries and developing countries are equal partners in agreements designed to bolster the economies of all the member

Box 1.1 Recent Regional Integration Agreements

EU HAS PLAYED A LARGE ROLE IN THE RECENT SURGE of activity, with the implementation of the Single Market Program in 1992, enlargement of its membership, and numerous agreements with other countries. These agreements account for two-thirds of the agreements notified to GATT/WTO since 1990 and include the European Economic Area, the Europe Agreements with the countries of Eastern Europe, the EU-Turkey customs union, and the development of a Mediterranean policy potentially incorporating regional agreements with most countries on the southern and eastern shores of the Mediterranean.

In Latin America, MERCOSUR was formed in 1991 and the Group of Three in 1995. The Andean Pact and Central American Common Market (CACM) were resurrected in 1991 and 1993, respectively.

In Sub-Saharan Africa, the blocs in West Africa were reformed and reorganized. The Southern African Development Community (SADC) developed out of an earlier defense-based organization, Southern African Development Coordination Conference, and was supplemented—for many of its members—by the Cross-Border Initiative. The East African Cooperation sprang up where the East African Community had failed.

The Middle East witnessed the development of the Gulf Cooperation Council (GCC), and in 1997 Arab League members agreed to cut trade barriers over a 10-year period. In Asia, the Association of Southeast Asian Nations (ASEAN) countries developed 25 years of political cooperation into a free trade area in 1992, with the formation of the ASEAN Free Trade Area. The South Asian Association for Regional Cooperation agreed in 1997 to transform itself into the South Asian Free Trade Area becoming, in terms of the population it represents, the world's largest regional agreement.

New ground was broken in 1994 when the Canada–U.S. Free Trade Area was extended to Mexico through NAFTA. For the first time a developing country joined industrial countries as an equal partner in a trade bloc designed to bolster economic development in all three economies. Links between high-income and developing countries were also being forged in the Asia Pacific Economic Cooperation (APEC), established in 1989—a looser organization, committed to trade liberalization, on a nonpreferential basis, by 2010 for industrial country members and 2020 for developing countries.

countries.[4] Perhaps the most important example of this is the North American Free Trade Area (NAFTA), formed in 1994 when the Canada-U. S. Free Trade Agreement was extended to Mexico. EU has linked with the transition economies of Eastern Europe through the Europe Agreements, and has developed the EU-Turkey customs union and a Mediterranean policy potentially incorporating agreements with nearly every Mediterranean country. There has been discussion of replacing the EU's trade preferences of the Lomé agreements with reciprocal trade agreements with these developing countries.

These developments have occurred against the backdrop of globalization. New technologies and more liberal trading regimes have led to increased trade volumes, larger investment flows, and increasingly footloose

Table 1.1 Membership of Selected Major Regional Integration Agreements (RIAs) and Date of Formation

Industrial and developing economies	*European Union (EU):* formerly European Economic Community (EEC) and European Community, *1957:* Belgium, France, the Federal Republic of Germany, Italy, Luxembourg, the Netherlands; *1973:* Denmark, Ireland, United Kingdom; *1981:* Greece; *1986:* Portugal, Spain; *1995:* Austria, Finland, Sweden.
	European Economic Area: 1994: EU, Iceland, Liechtenstein, Norway.
	Euro-Mediterranean Economic Area (Euro-Maghreb): Bilateral agreements, *1995:* EU and Tunisia; *1996:* EU and Morocco.
	EU bilateral agreements with Eastern Europe: 1994: EC and Hungary, Poland; *1995:* European Community and Bulgaria, Romania, Estonia, Latvia, Lithuania, Czech Republic, Slovak Republic, Slovenia.
	Canada-U.S. Free Trade Area: 1988: Canada, United States.
	North American Free Trade Area (NAFTA): 1994: Canada, Mexico, United States.
	Asia Pacific Economic Cooperation (APEC): 1989: Australia, Brunei Darussalam, Canada, Indonesia, Japan, Malaysia, New Zealand, Philippines, the Republic of Korea, Singapore, Thailand, United States; *1991:* China, Hong Kong (China), Taiwan (China); *1993:* Mexico, Papua New Guinea; *1994:* Chile; *1998:* Peru, Russia, Vietnam.
Latin America and the Caribbean	*Andean Pact: 1969:* revived in 1991, Bolivia, Colombia, Ecuador, Peru, Venezuela.
	Central American Common Market (CACM): 1960: revived in 1993, El Salvador, Guatemala, Honduras, Nicaragua; *1962:* Costa Rica.
	Southern Cone Common Market (Mercado Común del Sur—MERCOSUR): 1991: Argentina, Brazil, Paraguay, Uruguay.
	Group of Three: 1995: Colombia, Mexico, Venezuela.
	Latin American Integration Association (LAIA): formerly Latin American Free Trade Area, *1960:* revived 1980, Mexico, Argentina, Bolivia, Brazil, Chile, Colombia, Ecuador, Paraguay, Peru, Uruguay, Venezuela.
	Caribbean Community and Common Market (CARICOM): 1973: Antigua and Barbuda, Barbados, Jamaica, St. Kitts and Nevis, Trinidad and Tobago; *1974:* Belize, Dominica, Grenada, Montserrat, St. Lucia, St. Vincent and the Grenadines; *1983:* The Bahamas (part of the Caribbean Community but not of the Common Market).
Sub-Saharan Africa	*Cross-Border Initiative: 1992:* Burundi, Comoros, Kenya, Madagascar, Malawi, Mauritius, Namibia, Rwanda, Seychelles, Swaziland, Tanzania, Uganda, Zambia, Zimbabwe.
	East African Cooperation: 1967: formerly East African Community, broke up in 1977 and recently revived, Kenya, Tanzania, Uganda.
	Economic and Monetary Community of Central Africa: 1994: formerly Union Douanière et Economique de l'Afrique Centrale, *1966:* Cameroon, Central African Republic, Chad, Congo, Gabon; *1989:* Equatorial Guinea.
	Economic Community of West African States (ECOWAS): 1975: Benin, Burkina Faso, Cape Verde, Côte d'Ivoire, Gambia, Ghana, Guinea, Guinea-Bissau, Liberia, Mali, Mauritania, Niger, Nigeria, Senegal, Sierra Leone, Togo.
	Common Market for Eastern and Southern Africa: 1993: Angola, Burundi, Comoros, Djibouti, Egypt, Ethiopia, Kenya, Lesotho, Malawi, Mauritius, Mozambique, Rwanda, Somalia, Sudan, Swaziland, Tanzania, Uganda, Zambia, Zimbabwe.

(Table continues on the following page.)

Table 1.1 (continued)

	Indian Ocean Commission: 1984: Comoros, Madagascar, Mauritius, Seychelles.
	Southern African Development Community (SADC): 1980: formerly known as the Southern African Development Coordination Conference, Angola, Botswana, Lesotho, Malawi, Mozambique, Swaziland, Tanzania, Zambia, Zimbabwe; *1990:* Namibia; *1994:* South Africa; *1995:* Mauritius; *1998:* Democratic Republic of the Congo, Seychelles.
	Economic Community of West Africa: 1973: revived in 1994 as West African Economic and Monetary Unit, Benin, Burkino Faso, Côte d'Ivoire, Mali, Mauritania, Niger, Senegal.
	West African Economic and Monetary Union: 1994: Benin, Burkina Faso, Côte d'Ivoire, Mali, Niger, Senegal, Togo, *1997:* Guinea-Bissau.
	Southern African Customs Union (SACU): 1910: Botswana, Lesotho, Namibia, South Africa, Swaziland.
	Economic Community of the Countries of the Great Lakes: 1976: Burundi, Rwanda, Democratic Republic of the Congo.
Middle East and Asia	*Association of Southeast Asian Nations (ASEAN): 1967:* ASEAN Free Trade Area was created in 1992, Indonesia, Malaysia, Philippines, Singapore, Thailand; *1984:* Brunei Darussalam; *1995:* Vietnam; *1997:* Myanmar, Lao People's Democratic Republic; *1999:* Cambodia.
	Gulf Cooperation Council (GCC): 1981: Bahrain, Kuwait, Oman, Qatar, Saudi Arabia, the United Arab Emirates.
	South Asian Association for Regional Cooperation: 1985: Bangladesh, Bhutan, India, Maldives, Nepal, Pakistan, Sri Lanka.

Source: WTO data.

production. All these considerations point to the need for a new analysis of regional integration agreements—one that takes into account political as well as economic effects, that assesses the opportunities for deep integration, and captures the new potentials created by North-South agreements.

This Report

NO COUNTRY IS IMMUNE FROM THE EFFECTS OF regionalism as it shapes world economic and political relationships and influences the development of the multilateral trading system, and all countries face policy choices concerned with regionalism. Should they enter a regional integration agreement? With what other countries? What measures should be implemented— simple trade liberalization or deeper harmonization of domestic policies? There are no simple answers to these questions. Countries differ in their circumstances and in their political and economic objectives. Nevertheless, the economic tradeoffs that they face in making these choices can be identified and the process of decisionmaking made better informed. This is the objective of this report. We use the latest research on regionalism—research undertaken in the World Bank and elsewhere— to evaluate the experience of existing regional integration agreements and to draw inferences from this for the tradeoffs faced by decisionmakers.

An important question in analyzing the effects of RIAs is: Compared to what? The choice of counterfactual—including the status quo, unilateral trade liberalization, or multilateral liberalization—depends on the objective of the analysis. Answers will vary according to the choice of counterfactual. In fact, disagreements between policymakers or analysts may be due as much to differences in counterfactuals they have in mind as to differences in views. It is therefore important to be clear about the counterfactual that is being used as the basis for the analysis.

Given the wave of new RIAs in the last decade, and the fact that many developing countries have approached the World Bank for technical support and policy advice on whether to join or form a RIA, on the choice of partner, on the type of RIA, and on details of implementation, we choose the status quo as the counterfactual. However, when appropriate, we will also compare our results with those obtained under unilateral trade liberalization.

Politics and Policymaking

Many of the arguments for membership in a regional agreement are political, and we address these in the next chapter. There are three main issues. The first issue is security. There may be perceived benefits from using a regional agreement as a basis for increasing security against nonmembers, and there are some examples where this has occurred. A regional agreement may also enhance a country's security in its relationship with other members, an important argument in the early days of European integration. These security arguments are driven by a variety of mechanisms. Interlocking economies can make conflict more expensive; regular political contact can build trust and facilitate other forms of cross-border cooperation. But a regional agreement can also create internal tensions, particularly if driven by economic rather than security considerations and if the economics appears to bring an unfair distribution of benefits. History provides examples where this has led to the breakup of economic unions and to conflict.

The second sort of political effect is bargaining power—the hope that from unity comes strength. The likelihood of this occurring depends on who the member countries are. The EU has probably been able to secure more in some international negotiations than could its member states acting independently. Regional agreements between small developing countries cannot aspire to the EU's economic weight or political power, but can nevertheless enter negotiations more effectively than separate countries might be able to. They are more likely to "be noticed," and thence more likely to be able to make deals. Of course, these benefits depend on members being able to formulate a common position on relevant issues, a goal that has often proved elusive.

The third issue is "lock-in," and relates to the effect of the regional agreement on domestic politics. Attempts at reform are often under-mined by expectations of reversal. A regional agreement can provide a "commitment mechanism" for trade and other policy reform measures. It can be a way of raising the cost, and thereby reducing the likelihood, of policy reversal. This argument can apply to political as well as eco-nomic reform, and there are examples where regional integration agree-ments have reinforced democracy in member states. However, the effec-tiveness of regional agreements as "commitment mechanisms" depends on the interests and degree of involvement of all the countries concerned. Domestic political pressures and the activities of lobbies will also influ-ence the form of many regional agreements—quite possibly preventing them from being as effective as they might otherwise have been.

Economic Costs and Benefits

The economic effects of regional agreements are studied in chapter 3, and are of two main types. The first are "scale and competition" effects. Removal of trade barriers is like a market enlargement, as separate na-tional markets move toward integration in a regional market. This allows firms to benefit from greater scale and attracts investment projects for which market size is important, including foreign direct investment (FDI). Removing barriers also forces firms from different member countries into closer competition with each other, possibly inducing them to make effi-ciency improvements. Although these are major sources of benefit, we will see that the effects are not always achieved, and that the effects depend on the design and implementation of the agreement. Some of these benefits may be achievable with unilateral trade liberalization, although the latter may not always be politically feasible.

The second source of economic change is "trade and location" effects. The preferential reduction in tariffs within a regional agreement will induce purchasers to switch demand toward supply from partner countries, at the expense of both domestic production and imports from nonmembers. This is trade creation and trade diversion. Governments will lose tariff revenue, and the overall effect on national income may be positive or negative, depending on the costs of alternative sources of supply and on trade policy toward nonmember countries.

Changes in trade flows induce changes in the location of production between member countries of a regional agreement. These relocations are determined by the comparative advantage of member countries, by agglomeration or clustering effects, and by possible technology transfer between countries. In some circumstances, relocations can be a force for convergence of income levels between countries. Labor-intensive production activities may move toward lower-wage countries, raising wages there. In other circumstances, relocations can be a force for divergence. Industry may be pulled toward a country with a head start or with some natural advantage, driving up incomes ahead of other countries. We argue that divergence is more likely in "South-South'" regional agreement schemes between economically small low-income countries. It can create tensions that lead to failure of the agreement. "North-South" regional agreements are also more likely to generate useful technology transfers for Southern members, particularly if the Northern member is an important producer of knowledge.

Policy Choices

Regionalism confronts countries with four broad areas of policy choice; analysis of these choices is the subject of chapter 4. The first choice is with whom, if anyone, to form an agreement. A developing country may face options ranging from an agreement with another low-income country, to partnership with a high-income country or bloc, or membership of a large regional grouping such as the Asia Pacific Economic Cooperation (APEC). The political and economic effects differ widely across these cases, and we identify circumstances under which we think gains or losses are more or less likely. We also investigate the costs and benefits of belonging to more than one agreement.

The second policy choice concerns the policy stance members of a regional agreement take toward the outside world. A regional agreement is inherently preferential, discriminating in favor of members—how discriminatory should it be? Trade policy may be set regional agreement wide (as is the case in a customs union) or left to the discretion of individual members (as in a free trade area). These different arrangements each have costs and benefits, as well as creating different incentives for setting external trade policy.

The third area of policy choice is the "depth" of integration to be pursued. Different countries enter regional agreements with very different objectives and constraints. For some the objectives are to secure economic integration and to build deep political links, and there is a willingness to exert political effort to meet these objectives. Thus, the EU seeks "economic union" and the development of shared political institutions. "Deep" integration of this type may bring larger benefits in many areas of activity. For example, deep integration might involve harmonization of product standards and of parts of the fiscal system. This will make it more likely that economic "scale and competition" gains are realized. However, it also involves greater loss of sovereignty, greater political commitment, and far more complex policymaking than would a looser free trade agreement.

In addition to the depth of integration, countries must also decide on the "width" of an agreement, and this is the fourth policy area. How wide a range of activities should be covered by an integration agreement—just trade in goods, or also extension to services and factor mobility? We look at some of the economic issues that arise, and some of the practical problems that may be encountered as countries choose the depth and width of integration.

Regionalism and the World Trading System

One of the most hotly debated issues in the area is the effect of regionalism on the world trading system. To some, regionalism is a "stepping stone" toward global free trade, while to others it is a "stumbling block," inhibiting progress in multilateral trade liberalization. We address these issues in chapter 5, and find no evidence that regionalism has caused tariffs on nonmembers to be higher than they otherwise would have been. But neither do we accept the arguments that regionalism sets in train a "liberal dynamic," or facilitates multilateral liberalization. We find some case for strengthening the operation of WTO procedures to ensure that regional agreements are genuinely trade liberalizing, and for increased access to Organisation for Economic Co-Operation and Development (OECD) markets for developing countries.

The Scope of this Report

Although we argue that analysis of regional integration agreements should go well beyond traditional approaches of trade creation and trade diversion, we must also circumscribe the scope of this report. Our focus is trade, and we do not discuss either free movement of labor or monetary union. These are both features of the EU, but they are rare elsewhere. The EU is the only major regional agreement that gives all citizens right of abode and employment in all member countries. Monetary union occurs in francophone Africa, but it is outside the terms of reference of most regional agreements.

Notes

1.   This figure increases to 59 percent if APEC is included.

2.   General Agreement on Trade and Tariffs, which from 1994 onward has been part of the World Trade Organization.

3.   This model of "closed" regionalism was widely implemented, especially in Sub-Saharan Africa and Latin America and the Caribbean. Examples in Africa include the Economic Community of West Africa (created in 1973),

the Economic Community of West African States, ECOWAS (1975), the Economic Community of the Countries of the Great Lakes (1976), and the East African Community (1967). In Latin America and the Caribbean, examples include the Central American Common Market, CACM (1960), Latin American Free Trade Area (1960), the Andean Pact (1969), and the Caribbean Community and Common Market, CARICOM (1973).

4.   Unlike the preferential trade agreements implied by colonial preferences.

CHAPTER 2

Politics and Policymaking

Introduction

REGIONAL INTEGRATION IS GOOD POLITICS: IT MEETS political needs, such as security or enhanced bargaining power, and it satisfies influential lobbies. Indeed, the purpose of integration is often political, and the economic consequences, good or bad, are side effects of the political payoff. The most successful regional integration to date has been the EU. Here's how a president of the European Commission, Walter Hallstein, saw the balance between economic and political objectives in what he was doing: "We're not in business at all; we're in politics."

In this chapter we explore these political payoffs. When are they important, when are they illusory?

However, there is another and more worrying reason why regional integration is good politics. This is because those economic effects that are most apparent—larger markets and economies of scale—happen to be favorable. As we show, other effects make the net economic impact of integration ambiguous, but these are often overlooked in political discourse. So, regional integration is good politics partly because it is "soundbite economics," based on only those effects that are easiest to grasp. Sometimes the net effects will be highly favorable, but sometimes "soundbite economics" is seriously misleading: the illusion of gain collides with the reality of large costs and major redistributions.

The combination of political payoffs and soundbite economics is tempting, and goes far to explain the popularity of regionalism. Regional integration *may* also be good economics, but the impetus for integration has usually not been the economics. Sometimes, good politics delivers bad economics. The political payoff may nevertheless be worth it: If a country can substantially increase its security or lock in to democracy by joining a regional integration scheme, then it may be willing to accept a few hundred million dollars of costs as worthwhile. But sometimes the political benefits are ephemeral and the economic costs high. We show that the economic effects can vary enormously depending upon the characteristics of the country, the countries it chooses as partners, and the detailed design of the integration arrangement. Only by attending to these economic choices can the political momentum behind regional integration avoid the risk of driving an economy into costly mistakes.

2.1 Integration for Security

Intraregional Security

The politics that most concerned President Hallstein and his colleagues in building the EU was security. The preamble to the 1951 treaty establishing the European Coal and Steel Community, out of which the EU grew, stated its aim as follows: "To create, by establishing an economic community, the basis for broader and deeper community among peoples long divided by bloody conflicts." Written shortly after the third bloody conflict between France and Germany in 70 years, it was not surprising that security was paramount.

Security also played an important role in initiating regional integration in the Southern Cone. The Argentine and Brazilian militaries had long perceived each other as potential threats. Economic agreements covering steel and automobiles were signed in the mid-1980s as part of an attempt to reduce tensions, and the creation of MERCOSUR in 1991 reinforced this process. Rubens Ricupero, a former finance minister of Brazil (and now Secretary General of the United Nations Conference on Trade and Development) confirms the importance of MERCOSUR's security role:

> Both countries were emerging from a period of military governments, during which considerable tension had characterized the bilateral relationship... It was essential to start with agreements in the economic areas in order to create a more positive external environment that rendered it possible to contain the military nuclear programs, and to replace rivalry by cooperation (Ricupero 1998).

The political impetus to European and Southern Cone integration was thus based on the belief that increasing trade would reduce the risk of intraregional conflict. Similar motives are found in the creation of the Association of Southeast Asian Nations (ASEAN)(to reduce tensions between Indonesia and Malaysia; see De Rosa 1995), APEC, and the Central American Common Market (CACM), which include potential political and military opponents (Page 1996). Anwar (1994) argues that ASEAN has promoted regional peace, with intraregional conflicts among the five founding members before ASEAN was founded, but not afterward.

The idea that increasing trade reduces the risk of conflict has a distinguished pedigree. It goes back to Emanuel Kant's *Perpetual Peace* (1795). In the nineteenth century it was taken up by the British politician Richard Cobden, who put his belief into practice as an architect of the Anglo-French commercial treaty of 1860 (Irwin 1993). In the twentieth century, Cordell Hull, a U.S. secretary of state, also put belief into practice as one of the architects of the postwar international trading order. The idea turns out to be supported by some evidence. Polachek (1992, 1997) used the Conflict and Peace Data Bank to investigate both the association between trade and security and the direction of causation. He found that a doubling of trade between two countries lowers the risk of conflict between them by around 17 percent.

There are various reasons why this might happen. Political scientists suggest that negotiations between political leaders on trade issues gradually build trust, so that elites learn to form cross-national coalitions for subsequent collaboration. The founding fathers of the European Community, Robert Schuman and Jean Monnet, went further. They considered that economic integration would make war "materially impossible," meaning that interlocking of steel, coal, and other strategic industries would leave countries unable to wage war against each other (Milward 1984).

Thus, regions that are economically highly integrated may tend to have less internal conflict. It seems an obvious step from this result to the proposition that policies that promote trade within a region will increase intraregional security. If so, regional integration may provide a first-best solution and external trade barriers must fall over time and following deep integration (Schiff and Winters 1998a,b). Sometimes economic integration paves the way for full political integration so that the risk of internal conflict is greatly reduced. An example is the Zollverein of 1834, a customs union among the then-numerous German principalities, which was the precursor to gradual political unification over the next 37 years and the end of intra-German conflict. A second example is the customs union formed between Moldavia and Wallachia in 1847, which led to the creation of Romania 34 years later (Pollard 1974; Milward and Saul 1973).

Unfortunately, the result that trade enhances security does *not* allow us to conclude that policies that promote trade within a region will necessarily improve the prospects of regional peace. Indeed, they may have precisely the opposite effect, particularly when enhancing security is not the main concern. This is because policy-induced integration promotes trade at a price. The tariff preferences that induce regional trade can create powerful income transfers within the region and can lead to the concentration of industry in a single location. The countries or regions that lose income and industry can be sufficiently resentful that separatist movements arise and the overall risk of conflict is increased.

A clear example of how trade preferences can trigger conflict was the American Civil War. The Northern states produced manufactures that they sold to the Southern states, and the Southern states produced cotton that they exported to Europe. Tariffs first nearly triggered civil war in 1828. The United States was already a customs union, but in that year the U.S. Congress, dominated by Northern interests, sharply raised the U.S. import duty on manufactures. This increased the price that Northern manufacturers could charge in the South, and so generated a massive income transfer from the South to the North. The policy was referred to in the South as the "Tariff of Abominations." South Carolina refused to collect it and threatened to secede unless it was rescinded. The federal government sent in troops but Congress backed down before fighting developed. In 1860 Northern interests tried again, because the North had so much to gain from high tariffs. This time Congress would not back down. This (perhaps as much as slavery) was the issue that led the Southern states to try to quit the Union, and led to the bloodiest conflict of the nineteenth century (Adams 1993).

Protective barriers also played a role in the conflict in which Ireland broke away from the Union of 1807 with Britain. Although there were many contributing factors, the single most decisive was probably the Irish famine of the 1840s. As part of the Union, Ireland and Britain were regionally integrated behind high tariff barriers for grain (the "Corn Laws"). The Corn Laws enabled British grain producers to sell to Ireland at well above the world price. This income transfer from Ireland to Britain became most acute during the Irish potato blight because Ireland needed to import more grain during that time (Irwin 1996). Resentment at the profits from famine forced the repeal of the

Corn Laws, but not before mass starvation and emigration had taken place, sowing the seeds of future conflict.

A further example is the war during which East Pakistan broke free from West Pakistan to become Bangladesh. Here West Pakistan was equivalent to the Northern states during the Civil War, selling manufactures to East Pakistan at prices forced well above world levels by tariff barriers. When Pakistan (East and West) was created in 1947 the per capita income in West Pakistan was only 17 percent higher than in the East, but the differential grew steadily—32 percent in 1959–60, 45 percent in 1964–65, and 61 percent by 1969–70. Islam (1981) attributes the growing disparity to high levels of external tariff and quota protection, the concentration of regional development and investment in Karachi, together with the lack of labor mobility due to the distance between East and West Pakistan. East Pakistan's desire for secession was in part motivated by resentment at the large income transfers the tariff barriers created and this growing income differential.

Conflict within regional integration agreements is illustrated by the East African Common Market. In this case Kenya was the equivalent of the Northern states during the Civil War. Tanzania and Uganda complained about the income transfers that were created by the common external tariff on manufactures. They also feared that there would be increasing agglomeration of manufacturing in Nairobi, which had a head start on industrialization compared with the smaller industrial centers of Tanzania at Dar es Salaam and Uganda at Jinga. Arguments about compensation for the income transfers contributed to the collapse of the Common Market, the closing of borders, and the confiscation of Community assets in 1978. In turn this atmosphere of hostility contributed to conflict between Tanzania and Uganda in 1979 (Robson 1998; Venables 1999; and Schiff 2000).

In the CACM, Honduran dissatisfaction with the distribution of benefits was one of the factors behind the 1969 military conflict with El Salvador. After the war, El Salvador vetoed a proposed special development fund to channel additional resources to Honduras, prompting Honduras to leave the CACM (Pomfret 1997).

These examples show that trade policy can redistribute income and produce outcomes that worsen intraregional security. The genius of the European Community has not been simply that it promoted regional integration but that it did so without generating the large transfers that trigger conflict. How did the European Community avoid the problem? Partly it was a matter of negotiating style and partly a matter of detailed design. The style was consensual: negotiators always looked for compromise and conciliation. When a country signaled that a Community policy would cause it major problems it was accommodated, either by being bought off with compensation, as with the British budget rebate, or by being granted a gradual adjustment process, as with compliance with the rules on labor mobility by Spain and Portugal (Tsoukalis 1993). A key design feature that eased the problem was that the Community's external tariffs were generally low and declining. Hence, there were no large unfair income transfers with producers in one nation able to exploit consumers in another by selling at prices well above world levels. The one exception to this is agriculture, which has been very highly protected and which has generated large income transfers between countries. But the reactions to this exception support the idea that the transfers generated by high protection create conflict. Agriculture has been the most contentious of the Community's policies.

Thus, it seems that regional integration can sometimes promote intraregional security and sometimes worsen it. The net effect depends, in part, upon the economic characteristics of the members of the region and upon the style and design of the integration arrangement. Unless the economics is right, the belief that regional integration enhances security can indeed be nothing better than "soundbite political science."

Extraregional Security

The political impetus for regional integration is sometimes not *intra*regional security, but the need to unite to face a common external threat. The underlying idea is that common action in the economic sphere makes common action for security easier and more credible. The country perceived as a potential threat is typically the regional hegemon.

A good example of such a response was the formation of the Southern African Development Coordination Conference in 1980 to provide a united front among the small countries of the region against the apartheid regime in South Africa. Part of the strategy was to reduce economic dependence on South Africa both as a trading partner and as a conduit for the Southern African Development Coordination Conference trade with the outside world. Hence, an objective was actually to reduce trade with the hegemon (Foroutan 1993).

The Gulf Cooperation Council (GCC) was created in 1981 partly in response to the potential threat of regional powers such as Iran and Iraq (Kechichian 1985), and ASEAN was partly motivated by a perceived need to stem the threat of spreading Communism in the region. A major motive of Central and Eastern European countries in applying for membership to the EU is as protection against a perceived threat from the Russian Federation.

Sometimes regional integration combines the objectives of intraregional and external security. An example of how economic cooperation can be the precursor to military cooperation is the Economic Community of West African States (ECOWAS), originally formed in 1975. In 1986, 11 of ECOWAS's 16 members ratified a mutual defense protocol that authorized military intervention by the Community both in conflicts between members and if conflict in a member country was instigated from outside the membership. Clearly, 11 countries are unlikely to reach a military agreement without some prior experience of mutual negotiation and trust building. While the nations of West Africa have many subregional organizations through which they can build trust, most do not span the francophone-anglophone divide. ECOWAS was one of the few spanning organizations (Pomfret 1997) and so played an important, although indirect role in the establishment of the defense protocol.

While there is evidence that induced regional integration is a two-edged sword with respect to intraregional security, there is too little evidence to evaluate the effects on extraregional security. However, it is clear that security considerations of one type or another have often been an impetus for regional integration. The economic consequences of such integration are thus side effects of political decisions. A prime purpose of this report is to show how to assess these side effects. Sometimes the economic effects will be favorable so that integration offers politicians both political gains, such as enhanced security, and economic gains. Sometimes the economic effects will be unfavorable, facing decisionmakers with a tradeoff.

2.2 Integration for Bargaining Power

BY JOINING TOGETHER, THE WEAK CAN BECOME STRONG. JUST as workers band together in unions to increase their bargaining power against their employer, so small countries can band together to increase their bargaining power in trade negotiations.

How important has the motive of solidarity been in regional integration, and how effective is solidarity in trade bargaining?

The classic example of regional solidarity exerting economic power is that of the Organization of Petroleum Exporting Countries (OPEC). The OPEC agreement is not strictly regional and does not involve economic integration, but it does illustrate what solidarity can achieve. Its objective was not to increase trade among its members but rather to coordinate a restriction in oil export volumes, equivalent to a coordinated increase in export taxation. Hence, it was certainly a trade agreement. This was a successful bargaining strategy in that it raised the price of oil.

There is some evidence that one motivation for the formation of the original European Economic Community (EEC) in 1957 was the desire to increase bargaining power relative to the United States (Milward 1984, 1992; Whalley 1996). Some commentators argue that the formation of the EEC influenced the U.S. negotiating position during the Dillon and Kennedy rounds of GATT negotiations as the United States sought to mitigate the trade-diverting effects of European integration (Lawrence 1991; Sapir 1993; WTO 1995). The members of the EEC probably achieved two important bargaining objectives. They accelerated United States-Europe trade liberalization in manufactures; Europe is a net exporter of manufactures to America and reciprocal liberalization improved European access to American markets, and they delayed trade liberalization in agriculture. This raised the incomes of Europe's farmers at the expense of the rest of its population; although not good economics, this met the political demands of agricultural lobbies.

While this evidence for enhanced bargaining power may exaggerate the effects of integration, it suggests that there is indeed sometimes strength in numbers. How well might this result generalize to developing countries integration arrangements? We should expect that things will look different. OPEC dominated oil supplies. The EU created a grouping with a larger economy than the United States. No developing country regional grouping can hope to be in this league in terms of sheer economic power. In practice, developing country groupings have not succeeded in negotiating as groups. During the Uruguay Round, despite the existence of so many regional blocs of developing countries, most did not negotiate as a group. The exceptions were customs unions that, by virtue of having a common external tariff, are required to have a single negotiating position.

One reason why the regional blocs did not negotiate as single entities is that shared location often does not mean shared economic interest. The most successful negotiating blocs have been groups of countries with common exports, whether or not they were in regional agreements. OPEC is indeed an example of such a product-based alliance. During the Uruguay and Tokyo Rounds the most important such bloc was the Cairns Group of agricultural export countries, which had a common interest in achieving trade liberalization in agriculture and which was highly influential in negotiations.[1] It is suggested that it was only because of pressure from the Cairns Group that the United States maintained pressure on the EU.

Potentially, regional blocs can achieve a common negotiating position by logrolling, even if the interests of member countries differ. Each country agrees to support a long list of negotiating objectives—only one or two of which it has an interest in—to get other countries to support its own concerns. However, in practice, logrolling deals are easy for opposing negotiators to unravel by making offers that suit some members enough to tempt them to defect. Only if the parties to a logrolling deal are regularly making similar deals will they have an incentive to sacrifice the short-run gains offered by defection to preserve the longer-run benefits of cooperation.

The bargaining triumphs of OPEC and the EEC/EU are therefore a tantalizing, but ultimately misleading, role model for developing country regional groups. However, this need not imply that there is no scope for collective regional action. Even if a regional group cannot aspire to this much economic power, it can still work toward raising countries' visibility. After all, bargaining is not only about threats—it is also about the discovery of mutually beneficial deals. Even if regionalism cannot confer the power to be *menacing*, it can sometimes confer the power to be *noticed*.

In trade bargaining, countries win gains from an agreement by making concessions. When groups have the power to menace, they can use their power to make fewer concessions. However, paradoxically, when groups get together with the more modest objective of creating the power to be noticed, the ultimate test of success is whether or not they end up making more concessions. This is not because solidarity weakens their bargaining power: Rather, it is that if small countries act individually they may have so little bargaining power that they cannot negotiate attractive deals. They find themselves on the sidelines, with their offers of concessions seen as too unimportant to invite useful concessions in return. By combining their forces, they can cumulate potential concessions to a significant scale and so cut more deals.

The clearest example of regional solidarity with the objective of getting noticed is the Caribbean Community and Common Market (CARICOM), the alliance of small Caribbean island-states. CARICOM is not focused on achieving regional integration—rather its objective is common action. Without solidarity it would be quixotic for any single island to spend resources on international negotiations, and so it was evident that there were gains from pooling the costs of negotiation. CARICOM has been strikingly successful in getting its members noticed. For example, they have taken the lead in formulating and articulating the position of the African, Caribbean, and Pacific countries group in negotiating the Lomé Conventions. By pooling their support the CARICOM countries succeeded in getting their nationals elected to key international positions such as Commonwealth Secretary General and the African, Caribbean, and Pacific countries Secretary General. They also succeeded in negotiating a whole range of preferential market access arrangements with Canada, the United States, and the EU.[2]

Africa is the region most fragmented into small economies. There is thus a strong case for some cooperation in negotiations through bargaining units, whether through participation in product groups such as the Cairns Group, or through regional blocs. The national representation structure of the WTO tends to favor small countries, somewhat analogous to the United Nations, and so the existence of the WTO reinforces the "strength in numbers" argument for African collaboration. However, realistically the rationale would be to get noticed rather than to menace. Were Africa to use blocs to negotiate more effectively, it would be able to grant more concessions and thus cut more beneficial deals than it has done to date.

In one important respect regional integration can actually *reduce* the bargaining power of small developing countries. Consider the negotiation between a large multinational firm that is considering making an investment and demands tax concessions from the government of a small country. If the country is part of a regional trade bloc the firm can locate in any country within the bloc and still get access to the entire market. Governments within the bloc will tend to compete against each other to offer tax concessions: To each individual government a little tax revenue looks better than no tax revenue. By creating a regional trade agreement they set themselves up for a "race to the bottom." Hence, multinational firms can be expected to favor regional integration not just because it offers larger markets, but because it enhances their bargaining power. The only way for governments to prevent this effect of a regional trade agreement is for it to be extended to control such tax concessions; this goes well beyond the scope of most regional agreements.

A rare exception is a recent agreement on charges for cruise liners in the Caribbean. Until recently, cruise ships could discharge waste without charge at any island. Waste discharge inflicted cleanup costs on island governments, yet no individual island dared to levy a charge because the cruise companies threatened simply to divert their ships to other islands. In effect, the island governments found themselves stuck "at the bottom" in the charges race, because ships could choose freely between islands and each offered the same attractions. Analytically, this is precisely the same as the tax race within a regional trade bloc. Building on their previous extensive experience of solidarity, the island governments were able to coordinate the imposition of a cleanup charge. Despite threats of a generalized boycott from the cruise companies, the governments won their struggle. Hence, sometimes it is possible to counter the erosion of bargaining power that regional integration implies.

2.3 Project Cooperation

COUNTRIES CAN BENEFIT GREATLY FROM COOPERATION WHEN they share resources—such as rivers, fishing grounds, hydroelectric power, or rail connections—or when they join to overcome problems—such as pollution and transport bottlenecks. Failure to cooperate in these areas can be very costly. For instance, the uncoordinated exploitation of the Aral Sea by the five Central Asian riparian countries resulted in one of the world's worst environmental disasters, with the sea's desiccation, destruction of ecosystems, the pollution of surface and ground water, and more.

However, finding equitable ways to share the burdens and benefits of cooperation can be difficult. Countries sometimes find themselves unwilling to cooperate because of national pride, political tensions, lack of trust, high coordination costs among a large number of countries, or the asymmetric distribution of costs and benefits. Regional cooperation agreements are typically harder to achieve than national ones: they must be self-enforcing because of absence of regional courts or authorities to enforce them. The fact that these agreements must be self-enforcing reduces the set of feasible cooperative solutions and their benefits. International organizations, such as the World Bank—with high international credibility, expertise to deal with the complex issues involved, and the ability to mobilize financing—have often helped achieve an agreement where it might not have been possible otherwise.[3]

Regional integration agreements can help, because the ties of collaboration and frequent policy-level contact can raise the degree of trust among the parties. Moreover, regional agreements also help by putting more issues on the table and embedding them in a wider agreement, both of which lower the size of compensatory transfers required and make it easier to reach an agreement.

Regional integration was crucial in achieving project cooperation in the support the Southern African Development Community (SADC) provided to the Southern African Power Pool. The Southern African Power Pool provides for regional exchanges of electricity. Such pools offer large potential gains because peak loads do not always coincide, so that by pooling each country can meet peak demand while maintaining a smaller generating capacity. The gains over the period 1995–2010 are estimated at an astonishing $785 million, a 20 percent saving. However, cooperation is intrinsically difficult because each country has an incentive to underprovide expensive spare capacity, hoping to free-ride upon the spare capacity of others. Agreements can devise rules that forbid such behavior, but the rules must somehow be enforced. It seems that the framework provided by the SADC has provided this. The agreements between the EU and the East European and Mediterranean countries also include numerous initiatives for joint cross-border projects, covering transport networks, energy, environment, and other infrastructure projects.

Thus, though the support from the international community is often crucial for the success of cooperation agreements, regional integration is likely to help by increasing trust between the parties and by embedding the issues in wider negotiations where tradeoffs are more feasible and agreements easier to reach.

2.4 Integration for Lock-in to Reform

THE ARGUMENTS SO FAR HAVE ALL HAD TO DO WITH international relations, but integration can also help domestically, as a government seeks to implement its political agenda.

Reform plans can often be thwarted by the mere possibility that they will be reversed. Adjusting to reform typically involves investments, but these investments will not be made unless investors are confident that the reform will persist. Confidence in the persistence of the reforms may be low, particularly if the country has no track record of reform or, worse, a history of reversing reform. If the investments are not made, then government is likely to face increasing pressure to reverse the reforms—a "catch-22" situation (also known as policymakers' time-inconsistency problem). To escape from this trap governments often need institutions that enable them credibly to lock in to decisions. These are sometimes referred to as *commitment mechanisms*.

How good are regional integration agreements as commitment mechanisms? For trade liberalization, regional agreements are a well-designed piece of commitment mechanism because they are built upon reciprocal preferences: I reduce tariffs against you only if you reduce tariffs against me. As a set of self-enforcing rules this is quite efficient, especially if trade between members is large. The agreement reduces the likelihood of a country reversing its trade liberalization, because if it reneges on the trade preferences it has granted, it can be sure that its partners will respond by canceling the preferential access they grant. MERCOSUR provides a good example, where Brazil has had to back down on its attempts to deviate from the agreements after coming under pressure from Argentina.

Paradoxically, although regional integration works best as a commitment mechanism for trade policy, this is the area of policy where it is least necessary. This is because trade policy is the only area for which there is a well-established multilateral commitment mechanism, namely the WTO. Any country that wishes to reassure investors that trade reform will not be reversed can do so very simply by "binding" its tariffs to their reformed levels. This commits the country not to raise tariffs above bound levels, and is enforced by a clear and straightforward set of penalties. Indeed, a good case can be made that WTO enforcement mechanisms are stronger than those found in many regional agreements (Hoekman and Kostecki 1995).

But there is no equivalent to the WTO in other spheres of policy. Thus, regional trade agreements can be useful as a commitment mechanism if they are used as the foundation of reciprocal behavior on which other agreements are then built.

For example, the wave of democratization that swept the world post-1989 created a need for constitutional lock-in. Some regional trade arrangements have explicitly added a commitment to democracy to their original design. MERCOSUR put its—then informal—democracy rule into practice in April 1996 when the commander of Paraguay's armed forces was contemplating a military coup. The bloc's four presidents (with backing from the United States and the Organization of American States) reportedly quashed the rumored coup with a strong joint statement that democracy was a condition of membership in the bloc. Two months later MERCOSUR amended its charter to formally exclude any country that "abandons the full exercise of republican institutions" (Presidential Declaration on the Democratic Commitment in MERCOSUR, San Luis, Argentina, June 25, 1996; Talbott 1996; Survey on MERCOSUR, *The Economist*, October 12, 1996). In forming free trade areas with MERCOSUR, Chile and Bolivia accepted democracy as a condition for membership (Protocol of Ushuaia, July 24, 1998). However, this condition is only truly binding if the penalties for violating it are severe and effectively enforced.

Even without such explicit commitments, membership in a regional grouping can be understood to be restricted to democracies. This has clearly been the case with the EU, and the granting of membership to the new democracies of Portugal, Greece, and Spain is widely seen as an example of the use of a regional group as a commitment mechanism. We also see it with the eastern expansion of the EU, in which the EU Articles of Agreement with accession candidates are proving effective in promoting "full integration into the community of democratic nations" (Title 1, Article 2). For example, Latvia, which is a candidate for accession, is reviewing its citizenship policies for its Russian minority to meet EU concerns about human rights (*The Washington Post*, July 14, 1998). The preambles of the EU association agreements with Mediterranean countries include "the importance the Parties attach to the principles of the UN Charter, particularly the observance of human rights, democratic principles and economic freedom, *that form the very basis of the Association*" (Commission of the European Communities 1995, emphasis added).

Regional groups also sometimes use their potential as commitment technologies to lock in to economic policies other than trade. The most important example of this is probably NAFTA. Although NAFTA was ostensibly about trade policy, its underlying motivation was the desire on the part of both the Mexican and U.S. governments to lock in the broad range of economic reforms that the Mexican government had undertaken in the preceding years. The implicit agreement was that if Mexico maintained its policies it would have access to the U.S. market and also would have a more general claim on U.S. assistance (Francois 1997). One motivation for the U.S. government was that it had a strong interest in encouraging Mexican economic growth in order to curtail Mexican emigration to the United States. By making the Mexican reforms more credible it hoped to raise the Mexican growth rate.

Do regional agreements work as commitment mechanisms? The enforceability of bloc rules depends on both the value of belonging to the bloc and the credibility of the threat of action if rules are broken. If a country suffers little from leaving—or being expelled from—the bloc, then membership will not provide a credible way of committing to its rules. This suggests that regional agreements between smaller low-income countries, which typically trade very little with each other, add little to credibility (Collier and Gunning 1995). Credibility will be achieved only if a country that breaks the rules is likely to be penalized by other members of the bloc.[4] This will occur only if partner countries are sufficiently concerned to be willing to act to enforce bloc rules—for example, by expulsion or other sanctions. For instance, Mexican membership in NAFTA lent credibility to Mexico because the United States has a clear interest in a neighboring country with a pool of potential emigrants. But when members are more remote, engaged in less trade, or themselves less committed to the rules of the bloc, then enforcement becomes less likely.

Have regional agreements worked as commitment mechanisms in practice? For trade, the answer is broadly yes, although there have been reversals. Most agreements involving high-income countries have survived, successfully locking in their policies. Among developing countries the record is less good; a number of regional agreements have collapsed, or never moved far from paper to practice. When regional trade agreements have been used as the foundation for other types of commitment they have had some important successes, as shown by Mercosur's continuing commitment to democracy and Mexico's persistence with economic reform. Shortly after the NAFTA agreement in 1994 the Mexican peso was subject to speculative attack. NAFTA was evidently not sufficient to prevent this run on the currency. However, it probably was instrumental in determining the policy response of both the Mexican and the U.S. governments. Until 1994 the most common Latin American response to a major run on the currency had been to impose high trade restrictions and retreat into a controlled economy. This time the Mexican government basically maintained the reforms, although it raised some tariffs on non-NAFTA imports. The U.S. government also demonstrated that NAFTA meant more than just trade policy. It responded with a massive $15 billion rescue package, wholly out of line with its previous behavior.

In developing countries NAFTA is often seen as the model for a *continental* agreement. However, its true significance is not that it spanned a continent but that it spanned the North and the South. By using a major Northern economy that had a direct interest in its own performance as its commitment mechanism, Mexico increased its credibility. While there have been some attempts to create an equivalent arrangement between the United States and Africa, the underlying politics are less well suited. The United States does not have the same migration interest in the growth of Africa as it has in Mexico, and the U.S. market is far less important for Africa than it is for Mexico. A commitment mechanism for Africa that could be equivalent to the United States for Mexico is perhaps agreement with the EU, though there are some differences including the number and size of African economies and their distance from the EU. There are signs that Africa-EU trade agreements may in the future evolve to something more like NAFTA and away from the nonreciprocal concessions of past Lomé Agreements, although these agreements have recently been extended.

Thus, paradoxically, regional trade agreements may sometimes be more important for what they can do for the credibility of other policies, than for what they can do for trade policy. If governments want to lock in to trade policy they can most do so through the WTO.

2.5 Lobbying for Integration

GOVERNMENTS' POLICYMAKING IS LIKELY TO BE SHAPED BY the competing demands of different lobbies, which is why firms invest heavily in lobbying bureaucrats and politicians. Some interest groups will have much more influence than others will. Paradoxically, if the benefits of a policy change are spread very wide, no single beneficiary has an incentive to spend resources lobbying (an example of the "free-rider" problem). By contrast, if the benefits are concentrated, then it pays the few beneficiaries to spend heavily. Because of this, lobbies tend to promote policies that cause transfers from the many to the few, and this usually means that it is producer groups that dominate the lobbying scene. Usually also, producers competing against imports are more powerful than exporters; from a status quo with trade barriers, the import-substituting producers are already in business, while export sectors may be relatively small and undeveloped (Hillman 1989).

To producer groups, regional integration may appear an attractive option, particularly compared to unilateral nonpreferential liberalization. First, it limits the increase in international competition to which home country industries are subjected, since liberalization is only with the partner countries. Second, the agreement is reciprocal, with the home country obtaining improved market access in partner countries' markets. Since these markets also may be protected from competition from the rest of the world quite large profits may be possible; (we will see in the next chapter that preferential trade agreements can sometimes transfer tariff revenue from the government to importing firms). Indeed a number of authors have argued that politically sustainable agreements tend to be those that are "trade diverting"—maintaining high external protection, delivering minimal benefits to consumers, but raising returns to producer groups (Hirschman 1981; Bhagwati 1993; Grossman and Helpman 1994, 1995).

Political economy reasons may therefore make it easier for countries to liberalize trade on a regional basis than unilaterally, or through the multilateral process. Thus, for a government seeking trade reform, regional integration may be seen as the only politically feasible way to liberalize its economy, and perhaps also as the first step in a process of further liberalization. The former minister of industry in Morocco, Hasan Abouyoub, has mentioned (Abouyoub 1998) that trade liberalization would have been infeasible without first entering into a free trade arrangement with the EU. These arguments apply both for initial tariff cuts, and for the commitment not to reverse policy. We saw in the preceding subsection that it is possible for a country to use the WTO as a commitment mechanism, by setting its bound tariffs at low levels. But in reality many developing countries—including those that have made substantial trade liberalizations—have not used this option, but have instead left bound tariff rates at high levels, often much higher than actual tariffs. In a regional agreement the binding—to free internal trade—is reciprocal, and thus more acceptable to the lobbies that influence the political process. Olarreaga and Soloaga (1998) provide an empirical confirmation of this view for MERCOSUR.

2.6 Conclusion: So...Integration Is Political

TRADE POLICY GETS SHAPED BY THE POLITICAL NEEDS OF governments and by the political pressures exerted by well-funded lobbies. Adding a regional dimension to trade policy, meets some political needs and changes lobbying opportunities. Sometimes the political needs met by regionalism are highly valuable, such as the lock-in to democracy or to policy reform. Regional integration can also serve as an efficient tool to enhance security among member countries, as has occurred in some of the largest regional agreements. However, the political effects can sometimes be unexpected or opposite of the aspirations, as when regional preferences create such unfair redistributions that they provoke conflict.

It is not surprising if the economic impact of these policies, good or bad, is not very influential in the decision to join a regional integration agreement. Ordinary people will be made poorer or better off, but to date these effects have usually been incidental to the political debate. When regional integration makes ordinary people better off, the neglect of economic analysis does not matter. But sometimes regionalism comes at a cost. To know whether that cost is worth paying we need to know how large it might be. For this, there is no alternative but to understand the economic effects of regional trade preferences.

Notes

1. The Cairns Group consists of 15 developing and industrial countries comprising Argentina, Australia, Brazil, Canada, Chile, Colombia, Fiji, Indonesia, Malaysia, New Zealand, Paraguay, the Philippines, South Africa, Thailand, and Uruguay.

2. See Andriamananjara and Schiff (2000) for a discussion of the costs of benefits for microstates of joint negotiation.

3. The international community helped overcome seemingly intractable problems between India and Pakistan over the waters of the Indus River. India and Pakistan were unable to agree on a division of the Indus River Basin waters after the 1947 partition. In 1954, the World Bank proposed a solution based on dividing the Indus and its five tributaries.

4. See Fernandez and Portes (1998) for a thorough analysis of the conditions under which a regional agreement will enhance the credibility of policy reform.

CHAPTER 3

Economic Benefits and Costs

Introduction

MEMBERSHIP IN A RIA HAS IMPLICATIONS FOR ALMOST ALL parts of the economy. Some sectors will face opportunities for expansion; others will contract. Some sources of income will be boosted; others will decline. In this chapter we outline the main economic mechanisms that bring these changes and the evidence on their importance. We group these mechanisms into two main types, which we refer to as *competition and scale* effects, and *trade and location* effects.

Competition and scale effects arise as separate national markets become more integrated in a single unified market. The larger market permits economies of scale to be achieved and brings producers in member countries into closer contact—and competition—with each other. Entrenched monopoly positions are eroded, promoting efficiency gains within firms. Suppliers from nonmember countries will also experience the change in market size and competition, inducing changes in the pricing of their imports and in their attitude to foreign direct investment (FDI). We start this chapter (section 3.1) by examining these competition and scale effects.

Competition and scale effects can occur even if the sectoral mix of production in each country stays broadly unchanged. In contrast, trade and location effects arise when the regional agreement changes the pattern of trade and the location of production. The direction of trade changes as imports from partner countries become cheaper, encouraging consumers to substitute these for local production and for imports from the rest of the world—phenomena known as trade creation and trade diversion. These effects create real income changes for consumers and producers, as well as changing government tariff revenues. We analyze these costs and benefits in section 3.2.

29

As the direction of trade changes, so too does the location of economic activity within the integrating countries. Countries will see expansion of some activities and contraction of others. In some cases these changes may not be evenly balanced, so some countries (or regions within countries) will do better than others. Sometimes these changes promote convergence of income levels, raising income levels in poorer countries to the levels of richer partners. In other circumstances they may cause divergence, with some countries gaining at the expense of others. In section 3.3 we show how these location effects depend on the comparative advantage of members of the agreement, on incentives for clustering of activity, and on the potential for technology diffusion and adoption.

3.1 Competition and Scale

MANY COUNTRIES ARE TOO SMALL TO SUPPORT, SEPARATELY, activities that are subject to large economies of scale. This might be because insufficient quantities of specialized inputs are available, or because markets are too small to generate the sales necessary to cover costs. Regional cooperation offers one route to overcome the disadvantages of smallness, by pooling resources or combining markets. In chapter 2 we saw some examples of this in increased ability to undertake cross-border public sector projects. There may be similar gains to be had in the private sector, although they are likely to be achieved through quite different mechanisms, arising out of a combination of scale effects and changes in the intensity of competition. Note that the disadvantage of smallness can also be overcome through unilateral trade liberalization.

Domestic Production

Small domestic markets make it difficult to produce profitably goods that are subject to increasing returns to scale—declining average production costs. Even if production is profitable, scale economies mean that only one or a few producers can survive, typically with monopoly power, leading to high prices, low levels of sales, and perhaps also high costs. There is plenty of evidence of the relatively small number of firms operating in most developing countries, and Rodrik (1988) reports that measures of concentration (measures of firms' market power) in manufacturing sectors in large developing countries are typically between 50 percent and 100 percent higher than in industrial countries. However, entry costs may also be relatively low in developing countries, imposing competitive pressure on incumbents.[1]

What difference can a RIA make? In principle, a RIA combines markets, making it possible to reduce monopoly power as firms from different countries are brought into more intense competition. This can yield three types of gain. The first is the textbook gain from increased competition: firms are induced to cut prices and to expand sales, benefiting consumers as the monopolistic distortion is reduced.[2]

The second source of gain arises as market enlargement allows firms to exploit economies of scale more fully. In a market of a given size there is a tradeoff between scale economies and competition—if firms are larger, then there are fewer of them and the market is less competitive. Enlarging the market shifts this tradeoff, as it becomes possible to have both larger firms and more competition. For example, there might be an initial situation in which two economies each have two firms in a particular industry, and these firms exploit their "duopoly" power, setting prices well above marginal cost. After formation of the RIA this becomes four firms in one combined RIA market. This increases the intensity of competition, and possibly induces merger (or bankruptcy) of some firms, perhaps leaving only the three most efficient firms. The net effect is increased competition, increased firm scale, and lower costs. "Triopoly" competition is likely to be more intense than the original duopolies; and surviving firms are larger and more efficient, so can better exploit economies of scale.

The third source of gains comes from possible reductions in internal inefficiencies that firms are induced to make. If the RIA increases the intensity of competition, it may induce firms to eliminate internal inefficiencies (so called X-inefficiency) and raise productivity levels (Horn, Lang, and Lundgren 1995). Since competition raises the probability of bankruptcy and hence layoffs, it also generates stronger incentives for workers to improve productivity, and increases labor turnover across firms within sectors (Dickens and Katz 1987).

There is a good deal of evidence that general (nonpreferential) trade liberalizations achieves many of these gains. A number of studies have found that openness to trade reduces price-cost margins, an indicator of competitive pressure in the industry (Roberts and Tybout 1996).[3] There is also evidence of an association between trade liberalization and increases in efficiency, and between trade liberalization and a reduction in the dispersion of efficiency levels, as low efficiency firms adapt or are eliminated.[4] Tybout (1999) concludes that most of the efficiency gains from openness come from reductions in inefficiencies, rather than from scale effects.

When it comes to regional integration, we have less direct evidence. The most extensively studied RIA is the EU, and here the static gains from these effects have been estimated to range up to 5 percent of the gross domestic product (GDP), with additional, and even more speculative, dynamic growth effects on top (Baldwin 1989; Catinat and Italianer 1989; McKibbin 1994). These estimates are based on extrapolations of calculations from a handful of industries, and assume a significant increase in competitive pressure.[5] They are therefore appropriately characterized as somewhat "heroic" (Winters 1992). Even in the EU, there is some evidence that general external trade liberalization may be more important than regional integration in achieving these gains. Estimates from the EU found that procompetitive effects are largest not in markets where there is a high level of intra-EU trade, but instead in markets where there is a high degree of import competition from firms outside the EU (Jacquemin and Sapir 1991).

Turning to developing countries, there are several arguments that suggest that the *potential* gains may be larger than they are for high-income countries. The small size and relatively closed structure of many developing countries mean that there is scope for fuller exploitation of economies of scale and for removing local monopoly power. A well-documented example concerns duplication of plants in the tire industry of Central America (Wilmore 1976, 1978). A plant in Guatemala had the capacity to meet entire CACM demand, and there was another sizable plant in Costa Rica. Rationalization did not occur, however—possibly because the external tariff remained high, enabling the firms to impede effective competition. The service sector too offers considerable potential gains from opening to competition.

A number of studies calculated the potential (rather than actual) gains that might be expected from the competition and scale effects. Hunter, Markusen, and Rutherford (1992) construct a model of the U.S. and Mexican automobile industries and simulate the possible effects of NAFTA; they predict large increases in output for Mexico, increases in the scale of individual firms, and reductions in price-cost margins. A study for MERCOSUR (Flores 1997) based on a similar methodology suggests GDP gains of 1.8 percent, 1.1 percent, and 2.3

percent for Argentina, Brazil, and Uruguay, respectively (the larger economies gaining less because they are already closer to reaping economies of scale). However, these estimates are essentially predictions of what might be expected from regional integration, rather than measures of what was actually achieved.

The message from this section is then, that regional integration schemes offer developing countries substantial *potential* from these competition and scale effects. However, the gains are not automatic, and making sure that they are achieved involves careful policy design— and many of these gains can also be achieved through unilateral (nonpreferential) trade liberalization.

Market Segmentation and Deep Integration

The competition, scale, and consequent efficiency effects we have outlined are likely to be important sources of economic benefit, although they have proved difficult to quantify in practice. However, regional integration does not necessarily secure these gains. They arise from firms being brought into more direct and more intense competition with each other, and lower tariffs are a necessary, but not sufficient condition to achieve this.

There are some extreme examples, where RIA member governments, under pressure from industry lobbies, have deliberately acted to stop markets from being fully opened to competition. In Europe, a well-known example is automobile distribution, where a variety of nontariff measures restrict the ability of European consumers to engage in intra-European arbitrage. The measures include national product standards and licensing requirements that make it expensive for a consumer to import an automobile from another European country, and a tolerance of restrictions on competition in car distribution (Mattoo and Mavroidis 1995). In MERCOSUR, Argentina and Brazil have negotiated an agreement on automobile trade, whereby each individual *firm* is required to balance its Argentina-Brazil trade (Bouzas 1997). This inhibits efficient reorganization of the industry, and favors companies with plants in both countries, discriminating against other firms, and restricting competition.

Even if competition is not being obstructed in this way, it is likely that remaining border "frictions" will still create substantial obstacles to effective cross-border competition. For example, within NAFTA, evidence from Canadian-U.S. trade suggests exports from Canadian provinces to other Canadian provinces are some 20 times larger than their exports to United States states at a similar distance (McCallum 1995; Helliwell 1997); other estimates suggest that the United States-Canada border imposes barriers to arbitrage comparable to 1,700 miles of physical space (Engel and Rogers 1996). The significance of these border frictions is increased by the fact that firms will typically have no desire to compete more intensely with rivals in partner countries; they may seek to collude, tacitly if not explicitly, agreeing not to supply each other's markets. The implication is that markets will be left "segmented," rather than integrated into a single unified market. In this case the gains we have outlined above will only be partially realized.

This is one of the main arguments for pursuing "deep integration." Liberalization of trade between countries can involve not just removing tariff barriers, but also removing "trade chilling" contingent protection, and other obstacles created by frontier frictions, such as frontier red-tape, differences in national product standards and so on. The benefit of implementing as deep a range of measures as possible—and extending them into areas such as service trade—is that it will force firms to compete directly. It was precisely these arguments that caused the EU to embark on the Single Market Program in 1989—a far-reaching set of measures aimed at integrating markets (box 3.1). We return to ways of achieving this deep integration in chapter 4.

Importers and the Terms of Trade

If regional integration makes markets more competitive, then this should be felt not only by firms inside the agreement, but also by firms outside that export to the RIA markets. The more intense competition may induce them to cut prices; if so, this will be a direct source of economic gain to purchasers in the RIA (although the gain comes at a cost to these outside firms). The effects of RIA formation on import prices is an under-researched area, but there is now some evidence that they have achieved this effect.

Chang and Winters (1999) show that Brazil's membership in MERCOSUR has been accompanied by a significant decline in the relative prices of imports from nonmember countries. They use econometric techniques to investigate changes in the prices of U.S. exports

Box 3.1 The Single Market Program

THE SINGLE MARKET OR "EC-1992" PROGRAM AIMED at eliminating the remaining restrictions on the exchange of goods and services in the EU. The project involved adoption of almost 300 measures to eliminate intra-EU barriers. They fall into five main types.

- Simplification and in some cases abolition of intra-European Community border controls. This involves replacing border paperwork by an EU wide system of administering value added tax on cross-border transactions.
- Product standards: to remove the need for expensive retesting and recertification of products in each EU country, the "mutual recognition" principle was adopted, under which a product that can be legally sold in any one EU country can be legally sold in all.

- Progress toward deregulation of the transport sectors of EU countries, including measures to reduce restrictions on hauliers from one country accepting loads in another.
- The opening of public procurement in EU countries to effective competition from suppliers in all EU countries. Measures include the requirement that public projects be advertised in the EU wide publications.
- Deregulation of service sector activities, including opening financial services to competition and giving service providers and professionals the right of establishment in other EU countries.

Source: Pelkmans and Winters (1988); Pohl and Sorsa (1992).

to Brazil, relative to Argentinean ones. They observe a substantial fall in the relative price of the U.S. goods for most of the period. Formal econometric estimates suggest that these changes in relative prices are largely due to the reduction in tariffs on Argentine exports to Brazil compared to those on U.S. exports.

An additional test of the hypothesis is to see what happened to U.S. export prices in Brazil relative to U.S. export prices on sales to markets outside MERCOSUR. Figure 3.1 shows that U.S. export prices (averaged over 1,356 products) in the Brazilian market declined in absolute as well as relative terms over the integration period. Figure 3.2 shows a similar experience for Korean exports to MERCOSUR. These are sizable price reductions, and are confirmed by econometric analysis, which were also found for Japan and EU countries. They indicate that increased competition in MERCOSUR markets induced exporters to cut prices, thereby improving the terms of trade of MERCOSUR countries and yielding them a sizable welfare gain.

Is it necessary for Argentina to export to Brazil in order for prices to fall on exports to Brazil from the rest of the world, or is a *threat* of increased competition enough? Chang and Schiff (1999) find that the prices of

35

Figure 3.1 United States Export Prices to Brazil and Rest of World
(1,356 commodities)

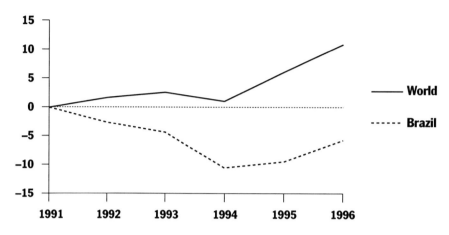

Source: Chang and Winters (1999).

Figure 3.2 Republic of Korea Export Prices to Brazil and Rest of World
(99 commodities)

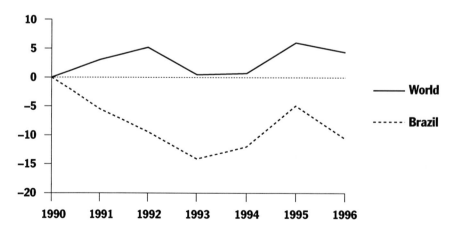

Source: Chang and Winters (1999).

exports to Brazil from the rest of the world fall even for products that Argentina does not export to Brazil, implying that the threat of increased competition may be enough to improve the terms of trade in MERCOSUR.

Foreign Direct Investment

In addition to changing the organization of local industry, if RIAs create large markets they may also assist in attracting FDI. Foreign firms that want to supply their product to a particular country face a choice between serving the market by importing or by building a local plant. The tradeoff is between the costs of tariffs and other trade barriers incurred on imports, and the production costs of the local plant. If the investment is "lumpy," requiring a certain minimum level of sales to be viable, then the scale effect of joining markets in a RIA may well tip the decision toward FDI. The decision will be tipped further in favor of FDI if the RIA makes the market more competitive, favoring lower marginal cost sources of production.

There is considerable evidence that RIAs—or at least RIAs with large markets—have succeeded in attracting FDI. Mexico perhaps provides the best example of this, although its position as a potential export platform to the United States is clearly special. NAFTA guaranteed market access to its Northern neighbors, and this had a profound impact on FDI, as can be seen from figure 3.3. Flows into Mexico more than doubled in the year following the launch of NAFTA, and Blomstrom and Kokko (1997a) argue this increase was mainly by non-NAFTA countries' firms taking advantage of preferential access to the larger Northern market. For example, Japan redirected part of its FDI from the United States and Canada toward Mexico, and many projects (in the automobile industry, for example) are intended for the NAFTA continental market.

Similar phenomena have been observed elsewhere. In Europe, a major surge of FDI accompanied the Single Market Program; the European Commission (*The Single Market Review* 4 (1) 1998) finds that the EU's share of worldwide inward FDI flows increased from 28 percent to 33 percent during 1982–93. In MERCOSUR too, there is evidence of significant expansion of FDI inflows. The share of the MERCOSUR countries in the stock of U.S. FDI increased from 3.9 percent in 1992 to 4.4 percent in 1995; the inflow to each country is given in table 3.1.

Figure 3.3 Mexican Foreign Direct Investment, Net Inflows

Current US$ million

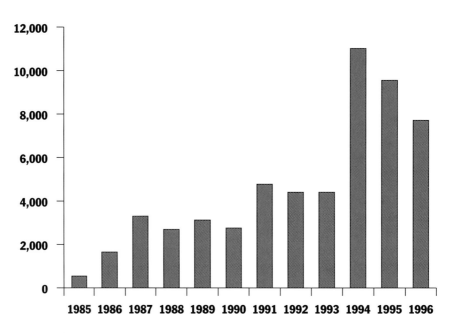

Source: World Development Indicators (various issues); Feenstra and Hansen (1997).

Table 3.1 MERCOSUR: Net Inflows of Foreign Direct Investment

(1991 US$ million)

Country	1991	1992	1993	1994	1995	1996
Argentina	2,439	3,934	2,421	2,843	3,774	3,781
Brazil	1,103	2,005	1,224	2,847	4,387	8,728
Paraguay	84	133	105	167	166	194
Uruguay	0	1	97	144	142	149

Source: World Development Indicators (various issues).

It is tempting to assume that inward flows of FDI are beneficial, although this cannot be taken for granted. External trade barriers can provide an incentive for FDI just to avoid these barriers. If the private incentive to undertake FDI is created solely by the desire not to pay tariffs to the local government, then this "tariff jumping" FDI can reduce real income, as it is possible that local production costs exceed the costs of imports. However, there is evidence that FDI can play a role in stimulating local production in related industries, in transferring technology, and in raising productivity in neighboring firms. (For a survey of evidence, see Blomstrom and Kokko 1997b, and Saggi 1999.) These benefits generally outweigh the costs associated with "tariff jumping."

Competition and Scale; Conclusions

Pulling together the strands of this section, we see that there are significant *potential gains* to be achieved, but that these depend on securing effective competition. It can easily be obstructed, and policy is required to prevent this from happening. We return in chapter 4 to a more detailed study of the policies that are needed if effective competition is to be achieved.

3.2 Trade and Location: The Pattern of Trade

REGIONAL INTEGRATION WILL CHANGE RELATIVE PRICES IN member economies. Imports from partner countries will become cheaper due to the elimination of tariffs, and in response demand patterns will change, causing changes in the flow of trade and in output levels in many sectors. What do we know about these changes, and what are their economic effects? These are intrinsically multi-industry or "general equilibrium" issues, involving expansion of some sectors, contraction of others, and relocation of industries from country to country. However, it is necessary to start discussion with the mechanics of preferential trade liberalization in a single industry—the analysis of trade creation and diversion first put forward by Viner (1950).

The classical source of gains from trade is that global free trade allows consumers and firms to purchase from the cheapest source of supply, hence ensuring that production is located according to comparative advantage. In contrast, trade barriers discriminate against some (foreign) producers in favor of domestic suppliers. This induces domestic import-competing producers to expand, even though their costs are higher than the cost of imports, which in turn starves domestic export sectors of resources, raises their costs, and causes these sectors to be smaller than they otherwise would be. Since a RIA liberalizes trade, reducing at least some of the barriers, doesn't it follow that it too will generate gains from trade? Unfortunately, as Viner pointed out, the answer is, "Not necessarily." The gains-from-trade argument tells us what happens if all trade barriers are reduced, but need not apply to a partial—and discriminatory—reduction in barriers, as in a RIA. This is true because discrimination between sources of supply is not eliminated, it is simply shifted. If partner country production displaces higher cost domestic production, then there will be gains—trade creation. It is also possible that partner country production may displace *lower cost* imports from the rest of the world—trade diversion.

Sourcing Imports: Trade Diversion

To understand the effects of discrimination, it is helpful to think through a simple example. Suppose that a country can import a good from a potential partner country at $105 per unit, and from the rest of the world at $100, and that in both cases the country pays $10 in duty, making the prices paid by consumers $115 and $110 respectively. In this situation consumers obviously purchase from the rest of the world and pay $110. If the country joins a RIA with the partner, imports come in duty-free so the price consumers pay for imports from the partner country falls to $105, while imports from the rest of the world still cost consumers $110. Consumer choices are obvious: They switch to the partner country, buying the $105 good and saving $5. But the government now loses $10 per unit (the revenue it was getting on each unit of imports from the rest of the world), so the net effect for the country is a loss of $5—the RIA has reduced real income. Another way of putting it is that the country (not the consumers) used to pay $100 per imported unit, and now pays $105. This is the deleterious welfare effect of "trade diversion."

This is just an example, and circumstances like this clearly will not apply in all sectors—there are some where partner country costs are less than are those in the rest of the world, and others where the country under study is an exporter—but the example makes an important point. Can we identify circumstances where trade diversion is more or less likely to be a problem?

First, notice that trade diversion can occur only if the country has a tariff on imports from the rest of the world, and that the cost of trade diversion cannot exceed the height of this external tariff. In the previous example, if the external tariff was initially low the loss of tariff revenue would be small, and if the external tariff were cut, the switch in supply-source would not occur. One clear policy implication is that member countries should lower external tariffs as much as possible.

Second, trade diversion arises only if partner country costs are out of line with costs and prices in the rest of the world, this will not be the case if the partner itself has low trade barriers. For example, if the partner had a duty of just $2 per unit, then prices and costs in the partner country could not exceed $102 (the price at which imports from the rest of the world would be sold in the partner country). Preferential liberalization would then cost the government $10 but save consumers $8, creating a net loss of just $2 per unit, and mitigating the cost of trade diversion. However, as discussed in chapter 4, the country with high trade barriers will impose rules of origin to prevent trade deflection (where imported goods are re-exported from the low- to the high-tariff country), and prices could still differ by more than $2.

Third, our example is of a rather artificial and "frictionless" trade; in reality products from different countries are not perfect substitutes, and trade faces transport costs and other barriers apart from tariffs. How does this change the situation? The fact that products are less than perfect substitutes means that the change in sourcing of imports will be less sharp than in the example, again mitigating the costs of trade diversion. The presence of transport costs means that countries that are close may have lower costs of supply than more distant countries. This is the "natural trading bloc" argument (Wonnacott and Lutz 1989; Summers 1991) and means forming a RIA with close countries may be less prone to costly trade diversion than forming one with more distant countries. This argument has not been resolved: the opposite view is provided in Bhagwati and Panagariya (1996), while Schiff (1999) argues that neither view is correct.

Trade diversion is more than a theoretical possibility —the best-known example is the EU's Common Agricultural Policy. This involves a price structure for agricultural products designed to divert consumer purchases toward EU farmers and away from non-European suppliers. Some of the money is a transfer to farmers' incomes, and some is, in economic terms, wasted, because food is produced which could be more cheaply purchased on world markets. Messerlin (1998) estimates the cost of this protection at, conservatively, 12 percent of total EU farm income.

41

An example from NAFTA concerns clothing. Following the "Tequila" crisis, Mexico increased tariffs on non-NAFTA imports of clothing from 20 percent to 35 percent in March 1995, just as it was reducing tariffs on NAFTA imports. Mexican imports from the rest of the world fell by 66 percent between 1994 and 1996, while those from the United States increased by 47 percent. Similarly in the U.S. market, imports from Asia fell while imports of clothing and finished textiles from Mexico and from Canada increased by more than 90 percent (USITC 1997).

A particularly disturbing possibility is that trade diversion may occur in capital goods or other goods used as inputs in production; this would reduce production efficiency, and possibly slow the transfer of technology to the country. For example, Madani (1999) examines the effect of intermediate goods imports in three Andean Pact countries (Bolivia, Colombia, and Ecuador) from the early 1970s to 1994. She finds that imports of intermediate goods from the rest of the world (primarily industrial countries) tend to raise growth while intrabloc imports do not have this effect. She also reports that the share (although not the level) of extrabloc imports in total trade has fallen, suggesting that regional integration might have a negative effect on growth. Her findings suggest that from the viewpoint of technology and growth, an agreement with a large industrial country is superior to one with a developing country.

Finally, note that a RIA between two small developing countries is likely to only generate trade diversion and no trade creation. This can be seen most clearly in the case of homogeneous goods. In each member country domestic consumer prices are fixed at the world price plus the import tariff. Since these do not change with integration, consumption does not change. However, production increases because each country can now sell to the partner without tariff. Thus, each member country substitutes cheaper imports from the rest of the world with more expensive partner imports. The outcome is trade diversion and a loss for both countries (Schiff 1997).

Exports and Trade Diversion

The focus of our discussion of trade diversion has been on imports. What about exports? Is an importer country loss due to trade diversion just the other side of an exporter gain, in which case the RIA as a whole would be better off? The answer to this is that there may be exporter country gain, but it is less, per unit, than importer country loss.

Recall that in our example above, consumers switched to imports from the partner country. Partner country export sales expand, but how much of a gain is this for the partner country? If exports are just selling at cost ($105 in the example), then selling more of them does not raise income in the partner country.[6] If, however, they are selling above cost, then there will be a real income gain. But how much higher than cost can the price go? The answer is that the price cannot go above $110 (if it did, consumers would switch back to buying from the rest of the world), so the exporter country gain per unit cannot exceed the gap between the price of imports from the rest of the world and costs (maximum $5 = $110 − $105).

This line of reasoning suggests another way of thinking about trade diversion. Returning to our example (for the last time), the government has given up $10 of tariff revenue per unit. We can see where this has gone: $5 per unit goes to the higher cost of producing partner country imports compared to the cost of imports from the rest of the world, and the remaining $5 is divided between domestic consumers and partner country firms, depending on whether these firms are able to raise their prices in response to having preferential access to the domestic market. It is often argued that an advantage of a RIA (over unilateral liberalization) is that firms benefit from preferential access to partner markets. This is true, but we now see that it comes only at the expense of consumers and government revenue.[7] The RIA acts as an inefficient way of transferring some of the country's tariff revenue either to domestic consumers or to partner country producers.

Transfers are important in North-South RIAs because developing countries risk losing from a RIA with the North. The reason is that developing countries typically have higher tariffs than industrial countries. Consequently, the industrial member is likely to gain more from increased access to the partner's market than the developing member. The latter can resolve this issue by unilaterally lowering its tariffs.

Government Revenue

For many developing countries trade taxes are an important source of government revenue, and membership in a RIA leads to loss of tariff revenue. This arises directly—as tariffs on intra-RIA trade are reduced—and also indirectly, when trade diversion occurs, such as when importers switch away from external imports subject to tariffs.

Loss of government revenue underlies the trade diversion argument, as we saw in the preceding subsections. However, if the government is constrained in its alternative revenue sources, then a loss of tariff revenue can be particularly damaging.[8] Many developing countries are heavily dependent on trade taxes as a source of revenue, with some African countries raising as much as one-half of government revenues from trade taxes. In practice, how much revenue has typically been lost by RIA formation? In many cases we see that larger amounts of revenue have been lost in countries that are less dependent on trade taxes. This paradox arises from the fact that intra-RIA trade volumes are typically very high in RIAs where dependency on trade taxes has been quite low (such as the EU), while countries with higher trade tax dependency have often formed RIAs with countries with whom they have relatively little trade.

However, there are exceptions to this. Cambodia derived 56 percent of its total tax revenues from customs duties prior to its entry into the ASEAN free trade area, with two thirds of these levied on imports from ASEAN countries (Fukase and Martin 1999c). Entry into ASEAN provided a powerful stimulus for the introduction of a value added tax in early 1999. In the SADC also, where some countries are heavily dependent on trade with South Africa, substantial amounts of revenue are involved. Table 3.2 gives estimates of the revenue cost of going to free internal trade, and we see that this will approximately halve customs revenue in Zambia and Zimbabwe, losing the governments 5.6 percent and 9.8 percent of government revenue respectively. These are very substantial revenue losses, and point to the need to ensure that alternative tax systems are in place before removing sources of trade tax revenue.

Trade Flows: The Evidence

Trade diversion increases intrabloc trade at the expense of trade with outside countries, while trade creation does not have this negative effect. If we look at overall trade flows, what evidence is there of trade diversion relative to creation? Looking at the raw numbers we typically see expansions both in trade within the bloc, and in external trade, suggesting

Table 3.2 Customs Revenue Collected as a Percent of Total Government Revenue in 1996 and the Implications of a Free Trade Area for SADC Members

| | | Estimated change in customs duty | |
Member country	Customs duty as percent of total tax revenue	Percent custom duty	Percent total tax revenue
Malawi	14.3	−36.7	−5.3
Mauritius	29.8	−18.2	−5.4
South Africa	3.6	4.9	0.2
Tanzania	24.0	−8.3	−2.0
Zambia	12.3	−45.3	−5.6
Zimbabwe	18.4	−53.3	−9.8

Note: The FTA assumes Free Trade on intra-SADC trade. The projections assume that each country's average tariff rates against SADC members are zero. There are discrepancies between the duty revenue reported by customs departments and that reported in budget numbers. For example Malawi reported FY96 duty revenues of 1,505.2 and 2,028.7 million kwacha against the 615 million reported by customs. For consistency, we have used the numbers reported by customs.

Source: Staff calculations, IMF.

that there is no evidence of trade diversion. However, looking at the raw data alone fails to distinguish the effects of regional integration from other economic changes—including in some cases external trade liberalization. To identify the effects of the RIA the researcher must try to control for these other changes, and this can be done with varying degrees of sophistication. When we include these controls we find that there is some evidence of trade diversion as well as trade creation.

The raw data on intra-RIA and extra-RIA trade for nine developing country RIAs before (one year before implementation) and after (five years after implementation) is given in figures 3.4–3.6. We see increases in intra-RIA imports for all cases (figure 3.4), although perhaps the most startling thing from the figure is how little trade there is within some of the RIAs; Union Douanière et Economique de l'Afrique Centrale (UDEAC) members partner trade as a share of GDP trebled, but only from 0.24 percent to 0.79 percent. For trade diversion, we look at the extra-RIA trade (figure 3.5) for evidence of declines, but here too we see increases, typically around much higher trade volumes. Looking at the ratio of intra-RIA imports to external imports (figure 3.6) we see that the share of intra-RIA imports expanded relative to external for seven of the nine RIAs (the exceptions are CARICOM and the GCC). However, since this was on the basis of rising volumes of both sorts of trade, it provides no evidence of trade diversion.

Figure 3.4 Intra-RIA Imports as Share of GDP

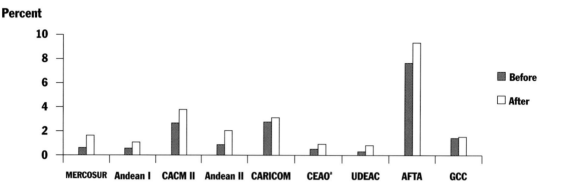

Figure 3.5 Extra-RIA Imports as Share of GDP

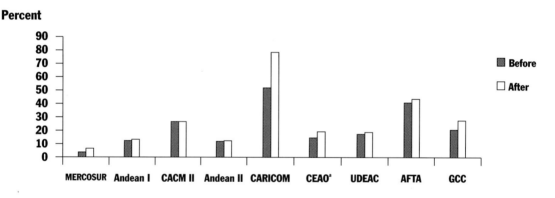

Figure 3.6 Ratio of Intra-RIA Imports over Extra-RIA Imports

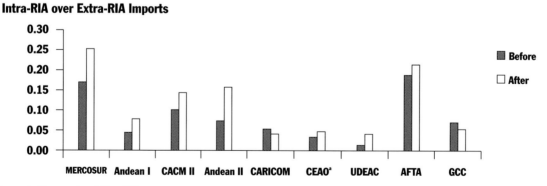

a. Economic Community of West Africa

Note: For MERCOSUR this encompasses two years 1991 and 1996; Andean Pact I 1968 and 1974; Andean Pact II 1990 and 1996; CACM II 1990 and 1996; CARICOM 1972 and 1978; the Economic Community of West Africa 1965 and 1971; AFTA 1991 and 1996; and the GCC 1980 and 1986.

Source: U.N. COMTRADE data.

The standard way to control for other effects is to build an econometric model of trade, and see whether the estimated relationships change as a consequence of implementing the RIA. The usual model for such purposes is the gravity model, which estimates bilateral trade between countries, generally for a sample of many countries and for several different dates. It explains trade between pairs of countries as a function of their GDPs (larger economies trade more), populations, the distance between them (as a proxy for transport costs, cultural similarity and business contacts), and physical factors such as sharing a land border, and being landlocked or an island. Researchers add to the list dummy variables that capture whether or not countries are in a particular RIA. If these show up positively for pairs of countries in a RIA, then they indicate that these countries trade more than would be suggested by the other factors. A fall in the value of a dummy for trade between a member and nonmember is indicative of trade diversion, particularly if the fall shows up after formation of the RIA.

Using this technique, Bayoumi and Eichengreen (1997) find that the formation of the EEC reduced the annual growth of member trade with other industrial countries by 1.7 percentage points, with the major attenuation occurring over 1959–61, just as preferences started to bite. Cumulating the decline in growth over 1957–73 gives lost exports to the rest of the world of $24 billion in 1973.

A recent example of this approach is work undertaken by the World Bank investigating nine major blocs over 1980–96 (Soloaga and Winters 1999a,b). Figures 3.7a and 3.7b summarize the estimates of the trade effects in 1980–82, 1986–88, and 1995–96. A positive value on the vertical axis of these figures indicates that a country is trading more than would be suggested by other factors. Looking first at figure 3.7a we see that the EU, European Free Trade Association (EFTA), and NAFTA had relatively high levels of extrabloc trade, but that these coefficients fell over the period. This suggests trade diversion was occurring. Surprisingly, the change in the coefficients on intrabloc trade are generally smaller, and in some cases negative.

Figure 3.7b looks at four blocs for which the picture is rather different. Extrabloc trade is generally lower for these blocs, but there is no evidence of trade diversion taking place during the period. Indeed, for ASEAN there is substantial increase in the coefficients for extrabloc trade, accompanied by a fall in that on intrabloc trade.

What do we learn from these studies? It is extremely difficult to control for other determinants of trade, but once we do there appears

Figure 3.7a RIA's Trade within and across Borders: Evidence of Diversion

(Gravity model estimates over three periods; 1980–82, 1986–88, 1995–96)

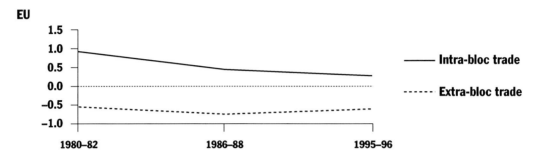

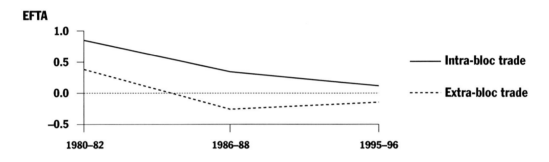

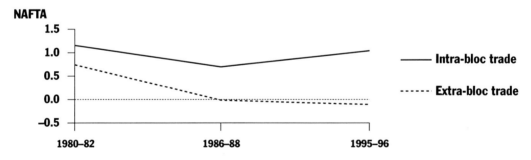

Source: Soloaga and Winters (1999a,b).

to be weak evidence that external trade is smaller than it otherwise might have been in at least some of the blocs that have been researched. However, the picture is sufficiently mixed that it is not possible to conclude that trade diversion has been a major problem. Furthermore, we cannot infer that trade diversion has been economically damaging without information on relative costs and tariff structures, which are not revealed in this sort of aggregate exercise.

Figure 3.7b RIA's Trade within and across Borders: No Evidence of Diversion
(Gravity model estimates over three periods; 1980–82, 1986–88, 1995–96)

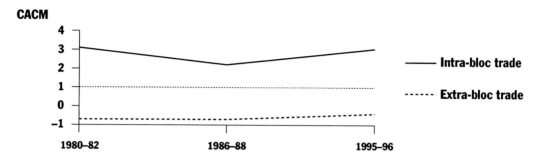

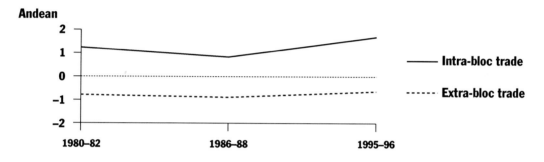

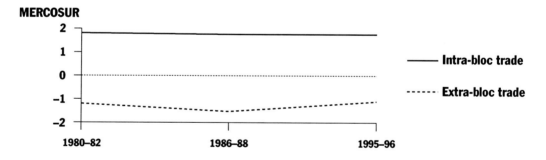

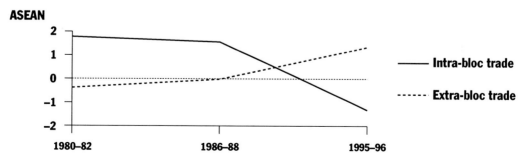

Source: Soloaga and Winters (1999a,b).

49

Computable Equilibrium Studies

Although the gravity equations control for some of the other factors determining trade flows, they cannot control for all of them. In addition, they do not contain the details about tariff rates and product supplies and demands that are needed to establish whether changes in trade flows are really beneficial or damaging. An alternative approach that enables the researcher to do this is to construct a full computer model of the economies under study, and then simulate the effects of the policy changes associated with the RIA. Such a model typically contains a great deal of microeconomic detail, so it can be used to predict changes in production in each sector and changes in factor prices and real incomes.

Models of this type come in increasing degrees of sophistication as researchers have refined technique.[9] "First generation" models assume that all markets are perfectly competitive, so the costs and benefits of RIA membership arise only from trade diversion and trade creation (the effects discussed in section 3.2). "Second generation" models include increasing returns and imperfect competition, so incorporate some of the scale and competition effects outlined in section 3.1. "Third generation" models contain some dynamics, allowing for capital accumulation, and sometimes also technical progress.

The conclusions from these models are, broadly, that there are gains from regional integration, but the gains are small (Francois and Shiells 1994; Harrison, Rutherford, and Tarr 1994). In the first generation models the interaction between trade diversion and trade creation brought effects that were typically very small—a fraction of 1 percent of GDP. Second generation models generally increased this somewhat, to around 2–3 percent of GDP. Third generation models increased the gain further, to approximately 5 percent of GDP.

The strength of these models is that they have sufficient microeconomic structure to enable the effects of a policy change to be traced out in detail, and its real income effects to be calculated. They are also often used for prediction—to estimate the likely effects of a policy change before it is implemented. But they have the major weakness that they are not usually fitted to data as carefully, nor are they subject to the same statistical testing as econometric models. The cost of the microeconomic detail is a complexity that makes rigorous econometric estimation impossible.

3.3 Trade and Location: Convergence or Divergence?

REGIONAL INTEGRATION WILL LEAD TO RELOCATION OF economic activity; industries will expand in some countries and contract in others, and as this happens demand for labor and real income levels will change. How will this affect member states, and which countries are likely to be gainers and which losers from this process?

There is an empirical paradox here that needs to be explained. There is evidence from the European experience that RIA membership is associated with convergence in the income levels of different countries. The overall dispersion of income levels in the EU to the mid-1980s has been studied by Ben-David (1993), from which figure 3.8 is drawn. The vertical axis of the figure measures the dispersion of income levels in Europe, and clearly shows an almost continuous convergence, from 1947 (when the BeNeLux Customs Union was created), through 1951 (the formation of Economic Coal and Steel Community), 1957 (creation of the EEC), 1962 (when quotas were eliminated), 1968 (when internal tariffs were removed) to 1981. Income differences narrowed by about two-thirds over the period, due mainly to more rapid growth of the lower-income countries.

The most interesting features of the more recent experience are the strong performance of Ireland, Portugal, and Spain, who have made substantial progress in closing the gap with richer members of the EU. Whereas in the mid 1980s these countries' per capita incomes were, respectively, 61 percent, 49 percent, and 27 percent of the income of the large EU countries,[10] by the late 1990s the numbers had risen to 91 percent, 67 percent, and 38 percent. This convergence did not take place in Greece, although it joined the EU earlier than Portugal and Spain, because Greece did not implement the necessary reforms after joining the EU. This suggests that even though integrating with a large and advanced region is potentially beneficial, economic reforms in the poorer country are needed in order to capture these benefits.

While European experience suggests convergence, the experience of most developing country RIAs does not. Indeed, there are several examples of integration being blamed for divergence of economic performance, such as the experience of the East African Community and East and West Paki-

Figure 3.8 Incomes Converge as EEC Integrates

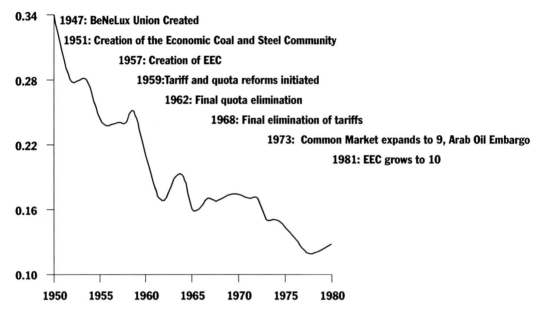

**Income differences
(annual standard deviations of log incomes)**

1947: BeNeLux Union Created

1951: Creation of the Economic Coal and Steel Community

1957: Creation of EEC

1959:Tariff and quota reforms initiated

1962: Final quota elimination

1968: Final elimination of tariffs

1973: Common Market expands to 9, Arab Oil Embargo

1981: EEC grows to 10

Source: Ben-David (1993).

stan, discussed in chapter 2. The concentration of manufacturing in the old East African Community (where the Nairobi region gained at the expense of manufacturing in Uganda and Tanzania) has been extensively studied (Hansen 1969). Uganda and Tanzania contended that all the gains of the East African Common Market were going to Kenya, which was steadily enhancing its position as the industrial center of the Common Market, producing 70 percent of the manufactures and exporting a growing percentage of them to its two relatively less industrial partners. By 1958, 404 of the 474 companies registered in East Africa were located in Kenya, and by 1960 Kenya's manufacturing sector accounted for 10 percent of its gross national product (GNP), against 4 percent in the other two states. The community collapsed in 1977, because it failed to satisfy the poorer members that they were getting a fair share of the gains.

More recent examples include the concentration of industry, commerce, and services in and around Guatemala City and San Salvador in the Central American Common Market (due to lack of data in the early years,

Costa Rica is not included) and Abidjan and Dakar in the Economic Community of West Africa. Figures 3.9 and 3.10 indicate how dominant these locations have become in manufacturing in their regions.

In this section we shed light on these differing experiences, by addressing the question, how can regional integration lead to relocations of economic activity between member countries?

Internal and External Comparative Advantage

To think about how industry will relocate within the RIA we look first at the comparative advantage of RIA members relative to each other, and relative to the rest of the world. It turns out that comparative advantage alone can go a long way toward explaining the different experiences of different RIAs, although these forces are augmented by agglomeration and technology transfer, to which we turn in the following subsections.[11]

Let us start by thinking of two developing economies that both have a comparative *dis*advantage in manufactures relative to the rest of the world, but the disadvantage is less for one of them than the other.

Figure 3.9 CACM, Formed in 1960, Manufactures Value Added
(percent of total)

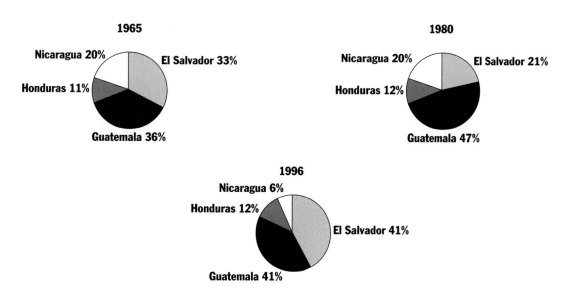

Source: Venables (1999).

Figure 3.10 CEAO, Formed in 1974, Manufacturing Value Added
(percent of total)

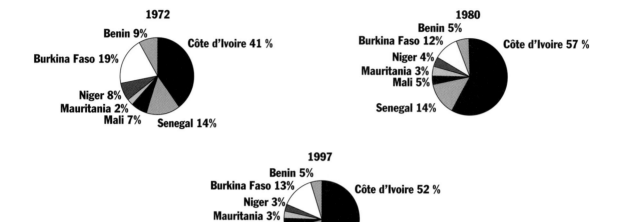

Source: Venables (1999).

Kenya and Uganda can serve as examples. Their comparative disadvantage in manufactures could come from many alternative sources—technological, geographical or institutional differences—but let us suppose that it is because of different endowments of capital: Kenya has little capital per worker relative to the world average, and Uganda has even less. The initial position is one in which both Kenya and Uganda have some manufacturing, serving local consumers and surviving because of relatively high tariff protection.

What happens if these two countries form a RIA? Since Kenya has a comparative advantage in manufacturing (relative to Uganda, but not relative to the rest of the world), it will draw manufacturing production out of Uganda, so consumers in both countries will be supplied with manufactures from Kenya. This moves Kenya's production structure further away from its true comparative advantage, while moving Uganda's closer. What are the effects of this on real income? Surprisingly, Kenya will gain from the relocation, and Uganda may lose (and will certainly do less well than Kenya). The reason is that Uganda is suffering trade diversion—some manufactures that were previously imported from the rest of the world are now imported from Kenya. But for Kenya there are gains from being able to supply manufactures in the Ugandan market, protected from competition with the rest of the world.

There is a general argument here, which is that countries with comparative advantage closer to the world average do better in a RIA than do countries with more extreme comparative advantage. Interposing the "intermediate" country between the "extreme" one and the rest of the world distorts the extreme country's trade, causing it to switch import supplier. But the intermediate country does not experience this switch in supply; its trade with the "extreme" country and with the rest of the world are less close substitutes, and therefore less vulnerable to trade diversion.

A further implication follows. A RIA between two poor countries will tend to cause their income levels to diverge, but a RIA between two rich ones will tend to cause convergence. The logic can be seen from figure 3.11. The vertical line measures each country's endowment of capital per worker; countries higher up the line have a greater comparative advantage in manufacturing, and also higher initial per capita income. For two countries below the line, we see the extreme country losing, and the intermediate country gaining—Uganda and Kenya, as marked. Similarly, for countries above the line, the extreme

Figure 3.11 Convergence and Divergence of Real Incomes

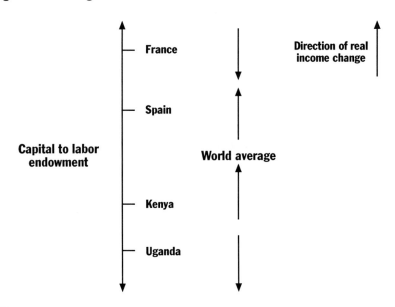

Source: Venables (1999).

country loses and the intermediate gains (labeled France and Spain on the figure). However, in the former case the extreme country is the poorer of the two, and in the latter it is the richer. The same basic forces therefore mean that regional integration between rich countries causes their incomes to converge, whereas integration between poor ones causes divergence.

The two cases analyzed above were for a pair of low-income countries and a pair of higher-income countries. What about regional agreements that link high- and low-income countries? The mechanism driving the changes is simply relocation of industry in response to differences in factor endowments, and associated differences in factor prices. The changes might be particularly large, and particularly beneficial, for a lower-wage economy in a RIA with an industrialized and high-wage economy. We have already seen how Mexico acts as a platform for FDI to serve the U.S. market, and there is substantial evidence of the relocation of manufacturing production from the United States to Mexico (Feenstra and Hanson 1997).

There is also evidence of a similar process underway in Europe, both within the EU and also in its relationship with some of the transition economies, with relatively labor intensive activities moving to lower-wage economies, and promoting convergence in wage rates. This may also become more important over time, as new technologies make it easier to fragment production processes—or "slice up the value chain"— moving labor-intensive elements of the process to lower-wage economies. Often this occurs through FDI, and within production networks, closely linked networks involving intrafirm trade, or trade between firms and established suppliers.

Agglomeration

Comparative advantage is not the only force that drives relocation of activity in a RIA. As economic centers start to develop, so "cumulative causation" mechanisms come into effect, leading to clustering (or agglomeration) of economic activity, and extending the advantage of locations that have a head start.[12]

Spatial clustering of economic activities is all-pervasive. Cities exist because businesses, workers, and consumers benefit by being in close proximity. Particular types of activity are frequently clustered, the most spectacular examples being the electronics industries of Silicon Valley, cinema in Hollywood, and the concentration of banking activities in the world's financial districts. Clustering also occurs in many manufacturing industries—for example U.S. automobile manufacturing in the Detroit area, or industries such as medical equipment, printing machinery, and others studied by Porter (1998).

Clustering or agglomeration typically arises from the interaction between "centripetal" forces, encouraging firms to locate close to each other, and "centrifugal" forces, encouraging them to spread out. The centripetal forces are usually classified in three groups (Marshall 1920). The first are knowledge spillovers, or other beneficial technological externalities that make it attractive for firms to locate close to each other—in Marshall's phrase, "The mysteries of the trade become no mysteries, but are, as it were, in the air." The second are various labor market pooling effects, which encourage firms to locate where they can benefit from readily available labor skills—perhaps by attracting skilled labor away from existing firms.

The third centripetal force arises from "linkages" between buyers and sellers. Firms will, other things being equal, want to locate where their customers are, and customers will want to locate close to their suppliers. These linkages are simply the "backward" (demand) and "forward" (supply) linkages of Hirschman (1958). They create a positive interdependence between the location decisions of different firms, and this can give rise to a process of cumulative causation, creating agglomerations of activity.[13]

These centripetal or agglomeration forces can operate at quite an aggregate level, or can be much more narrowly focused. For example, aggregate demand creates a backward linkage, drawing firms from all sectors into locations with large markets. Other forces affect broad classes of business activity—providing basic industrial labor skills, or access to business services such as finance and telecommunications. In contrast, knowledge spillovers affecting particular technologies, or the availability of highly specialized inputs might operate at an industry level. In this case the forces work for clustering of the narrowly defined sector, rather than for clustering of manufacturing as a whole.

Pulling in the opposite direction are "centrifugal forces," encouraging the dispersion of activity. These include congestion, pollution, or other negative externalities that might be associated with concentrations of economic activity. Competition for immobile factors will deter agglomeration, as the price of land and perhaps also labor is bid up in centers of activity. Also, there are demands to be met from consumers who are not located in the centers of activity; dispersed consumers will encourage dispersion of producers, particularly if trade barriers or transport costs are high.

How might the balance between centripetal and centrifugal forces be upset by membership of a RIA? Can membership cause, or amplify, the clustering of economic activity, and if so might it widen income differentials between partner countries?

By reducing trade barriers, membership in a RIA makes it easier to supply consumers (or customers more generally) from a few locations. This suggests that the balance of forces may be tipped in favor of agglomeration, although the ensuing relocation of industry could develop in several different ways.

One possibility is that particular sectors become more spatially concentrated, and this is likely if the centripetal forces act at a quite narrow, sectoral level. For example, industries in the United States are much more spatially concentrated than in Europe (even controlling for the distribution of population and manufacturing as a whole), suggesting that regional integration in Europe could cause agglomeration at the sectoral level (for example, Germany gets engineering, the UK financial services, and so on). The possibility that this might happen is generating some concern in Europe, although evidence for it is so far rather weak (see Midelfart-Knarvik and others 1999). If it does happen it will create considerable adjustment costs—as the industrial structure of different locations changes—but aggregate gains, as there are real efficiency gains from spatial concentration. This sectoral agglomeration need not be associated with increases in cross-RIA inequalities; each country or region may attract activity in some sectors.

An alternative possibility is that, instead of relatively small sectors each clustering in different locations, manufacturing as a whole comes to cluster in a few locations, de-industrializing the less-favored regions. Under what circumstances might this be the outcome? It will be relatively more likely to occur if manufacturing as a whole is a small share of the economy. This is because fitting the whole of manufacturing in one (or a few) locations is then less likely to press up against factor supply constraints and to lead to rising prices of immobile factors (such as land). It will be relatively more likely if linkages are broad, across many sectors, rather than narrowly sector specific. This in turn is more likely in early stages of development, where a country's basic industrial infrastructure—

transport, telecommunications, or access to financial markets and other business services—is thinly developed and unevenly spread.

This suggests that there is a real possibility that RIA membership could lead to agglomeration and growing divergence between member countries, as we saw in the examples earlier in this section. The agglomeration forces we have outlined here will interact with comparative advantage and may well reinforce each other. It seems likely that both comparative advantage and agglomeration are at work in some South-South RIAs. As Nairobi, Abidjan, and Dakar have attracted manufacturing, so they have started to develop business networks and the linkages that tend to lock manufacturing in to the location. The process might be further accelerated by the propensity of foreign direct investment to cluster in relatively few locations. Agglomeration is then accentuating the forces for divergence that we outlined in the preceding subsection.

In other circumstances agglomeration forces may pull against comparative advantage. For example, firms choosing location in Europe may want the agglomeration benefits of locating in Germany, but factor price differences create an incentive for them to locate in Hungary. An important final point is that agglomeration forces will be strongest at "intermediate" levels of trade barriers (or transport costs). When barriers are very high, each country will have its own industry to supply local consumers. When they are very low firms go where labor costs are cheapest, because they can bring in their inputs and ship their output at very low cost—as with the production networks described in box 3.2. But at "intermediate" barriers firms are reluctant to move away from suppliers and other agglomeration benefits, yet are able to supply foreign markets through exports.

Knowledge Flows

Both the comparative advantage and agglomeration mechanisms suggest that integration may cause the performance of members of developing country RIAs to diverge. One further factor needs to be added to the convergence or divergence calculus. RIAs may promote knowledge flows between member countries.

An influential—although not universally accepted—body of work argues that trade flows provide a powerful mechanism for the transfer of technology between countries. A good example of this are the works

Box 3.2 Production Networks

LOW TRADE BARRIERS AND NEW INFORMATION technologies make it possible to split the production process in many goods, relocating labor-intensive parts of the process to lower-wage economies. This has led to growth of trade in components, which now accounts for a substantial part of some country's imports (WDR 1999). Such tightly integrated international production chains are sometimes referred to as production networks.

Ireland provides a good example of production networks in Europe. Since joining the European Community in 1973 Ireland has attracted multinationals which use Ireland as an export platform to supply the rest of Europe. By 1993 foreign owned plants produced 60 percent of gross output and accounted for nearly 45 percent of manufacturing employment (Barry and Bradley 1997). They are concentrated in high-technology sectors, and import two-thirds of their inputs and export about 86 percent of their output.

Similar developments are occurring in some of the East European countries that have regional agreements with the EU, in particular Hungary and Estonia. Production networks are particularly important in the automotive, telecommunications, and office machinery sectors, and have accounted for a rising share of the trade of these countries.

of Coe and Helpman (1995) and Coe, Helpman, and Hoffmaister (1997), which seek to explain the rate of increase in total factor productivity across OECD and developing countries. They construct an index of total knowledge capital (measured by accumulated investment in research and development) in each industrial country, and assume that trading partners get access to a country's stock of knowledge in proportion to their imports from that country.

These authors find that access to foreign knowledge is a statistically significant determinant of the rate of growth of total factor productivity. For developing countries, Coe, Helpman, and Hoffmaister find that productivity growth is related to the interaction between the *openness* of the economy (imports relative to GDP) and *access* to foreign knowledge. Thus, an economy benefits from foreign knowledge, first, according to how open it is, and, second, according to whether it is open to those countries that have the largest knowledge stocks. These results are intuitively very attractive and suggest, again, that trade is a major conduit for spillovers between countries.[14] Of course, these results may be due to other factors highly correlated with trade, such as foreign direct investment.

Although the research was not undertaken explicitly for RIAs, it has clear implications. Increasing trade with high-income countries by forming a North-South RIA may lead to beneficial transfers of technology, and consequent convergence of incomes. Developing country RIAs do not offer such good prospects—particularly if they are relatively closed to external trade and cause trade diversion.

Convergence or Divergence: The Balance

We have seen how there are conflicting forces at work, some tending to lead to convergence of member countries, others pushing divergence. How do we think these forces balance out? In regional agreements that include high-wage countries with industrial centers and lower-wage countries, our judgment is that the convergence is probably dominant. But for South-South RIAs—particularly between the lowest income countries where manufacturing is small and business infrastructure thin—the analytical arguments suggest that there is a real danger of divergence. The analytical arguments are supported by the empirics, suggesting that RIAs containing high-wage countries have promoted income convergence, in a way that South-South RIAs have not.

3.4 Conclusion

A S POINTED OUT IN THE INTRODUCTION TO THIS CHAPTER, regional integration will affect many aspects of economic life. Whether or not trade diversion dominates trade creation depends on the specific circumstances. There is potential for gains from "competition and scale" effects in industrial sectors of the economy, but achieving these might require "deep integration" policies, and these gains might also be achievable through unilateral trade liberalization. The government will lose revenue, and some of this may be dissipated through trade diversion. Industries are likely to relocate, benefiting some countries and possibly harming others.

The ambivalence of these conclusions does not reflect ignorance but rather the wide range of country circumstances and policy options that exist. There are thus no fast and easy conclusions, but a number of reasonably firm policy conclusions are provided at the end of chapter 4.

Notes

1. Tybout (1999) fails to find evidence that price-cost margins are systematically higher in developing than in industrial countries, although reports a number of examples where this is so.

2. Djankov and Hoekman (1998) report the positive effects of trade reform on competition in Slovakia.

3. See Levinsohn (1993); Harrison (1994); Foroutan (1996); and Krishna and Mitra (1997).

4. See Nishimuzi and Page (1982); Tybout and others (1991); Haddad (1993); Haddad and Harrison (1993); Tybout and Westbrook (1995); Harrison (1996).

5. The original industry studies in this area were undertaken by Smith and Venables (1988).

6. Because some other sector must contract to release resources for the expansion.

7. Partner country consumers and government for exports; own consumers and government for imports from partners.

8. Any additional cost of losing government revenue applies only if the shadow price on government revenue is greater than unity.

9. This classification is from Baldwin and Venables (1997), who survey some of these studies in greater detail.

10. We use the average of France, Germany, Italy, and the United Kingdom.

11. This section is based on Venables (1999).

12. This section is based on Fujita, Krugman, and Venables (1999).

13. This argument only works if there are increasing returns to scale in production. (If not, firms can put small plants in many different locations.) For formal analysis see Fujita, Krugman, and Venables (1999).

14. The conclusion has been challenged because the paper assumes, rather than tests, that imports from industrial countries provide the correct weights with which to combine stocks of foreign knowledge. Keller (1998) has suggested that the results are little better than would be obtained from relating total factor productivity to a random weighting of foreign knowledge stocks.

Policy Choices

Introduction

W E HAVE NOW REVIEWED MUCH OF THE THEORY AND evidence on the political and economic effects of regional integration schemes. How is this discussion brought to bear on a particular country faced with decisions on RIA membership? What choices will the country face, and how should the theory and evidence inform these choices?

We group the choices under four headings. The first is who—if anyone—a country's RIA partners should be. The political and economic forces described in the previous chapters will have different effects depending on the characteristics of the countries concerned. Here we bring these together, showing how the effects might work for hypothetical pairings of countries. Related to the choice of partner are issues to do with the size of the RIA, and with multiple membership: should a country focus on membership of a single RIA or opt for many?

The second set of policy choices is to do with the external policy of countries in a RIA, which in turn depend importantly on the type of RIA that is adopted: a free trade area or a customs union. There are considerable benefits from merging external trade policy through membership of a customs union, since it allows freer circulation of goods within the RIA. However, it also involves greater loss of sovereignty and more political commitment, as well as possibly leading to the formation of new trade policy lobbies.

We then turn to the third and fourth policy choices, the "depth" and "width" of integration. The question is whether to deepen an agreement to cover domestic policies that affect the ability of consumers and producers to engage in intra-RIA trade in goods; and whether to widen the coverage to extend beyond merchandise trade. The tradeoff running through all these cases is between the potential for greater benefit from making the integration deep and wide, versus the considerable practical problems and potential political difficulties that may be involved. We look at a number of issues, including contingent protection, product standards, trade in services, and investment rules to see the benefits and costs involved.

4.1 Partners: With Whom?

SOME RIAS ARE JUST BETWEEN HIGH-INCOME COUNTRIES (SUCH as EU or the European Economic Area), some only middle-income (such as MERCOSUR or the ASEAN Free Trade Area), and some only low-income (such as the West African Economic and Monetary Union (UEMOA)). Others contain a mixture, often with a dominant high-income partner (such as NAFTA or the EU Association agreements with Central European and Mediterranean countries). RIAs come in all sizes, both in terms of number of members, and in terms of income; the EU has 15 members and GDP of US$8.4 trillion, while UEMOA's eight members have a combined GDP of US$24 billion; many RIAs are just bilateral agreements between a pair of countries.

In some RIAs most trade is between members, while in others very little is. We see from figure 4.1 that the 1996 share of member countries' exports that goes to other member countries is 62 percent for EU-12 and 47 percent for NAFTA. In middle-income RIAs, the share is smaller, at 23 percent for MERCOSUR, dropping still further for low-income RIAs, at 9 percent for ECOWAS and UEMOA, and only 1.9 percent for the Economic and Monetary Community of Central Africa.

While no single country will face a menu of choices containing all these possibilities, we want to show how the effects discussed in previous chapters apply to these widely different options for regional integration. We do this by considering some hypothetical country pairings, which are given in table 4.1. Pairs of country types are given in the columns, and our main political and economic arguments are in the rows. The country pairings are not to be taken literally, and the signs of the effects, which we give in the body of the table, are not drawn from research on the particular named economies. Instead, the country pairs are representative of types of RIAs, and the body of the

Figure 4.1 Intra-RIA Exports as a Share of the RIA's Total Exports

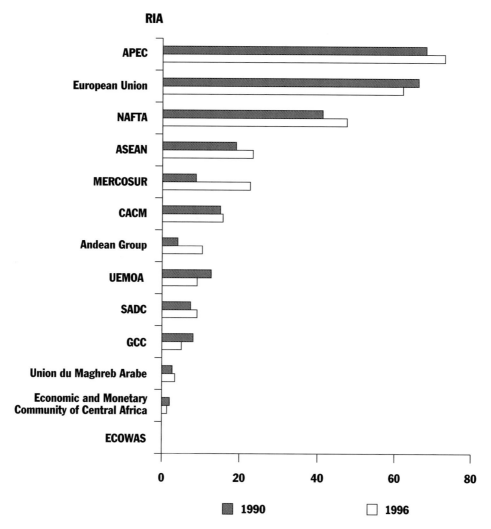

Source: U.N. COMTRADE data.

table summarizes our judgment about the sign and strength of the forces we have discussed in preceding chapters. The four country groupings we have chosen are therefore intended to represent a middle-income country and a high-income country—we label them "Poland" and the "EU"; two middle-income countries—"Brazil" and "Argentina"; a pair of small low-income countries—"Burkina Faso" and "Côte d'Ivoire"; and a small low-income country and a large high-income country or bloc—"Kenya" and the "EU."

Table 4.1 Pluses and Minuses of Hypothetical RIAs

Category	Poland	European Union	Brazil	Argentina	Burkina Faso	Côte d'Ivoire	Kenya	European Union
Political								
Security	+	0	+	+	?	?	+?	0
Bargaining	0	0	+	+	0	0	0	0
Being noticed	0	0	+	+	+	+	0	0
Policy lock-in	+	0	+	+	0?	0?	+?	0
Cooperation	+	+	+	+	+	+	+?	0
Economic								
Scale and competition	+	+	+?	+?	0?	+?	+?	0
Trade diversion	–?	0	–	–	–	–?	–?	0
Fiscal	–	0	–?	–?	–	+?	–	0
Trade and location	+	+	+?	+?	–	+	+?	0
Technology transfer	+	0	+?	+?	0	0	+	0

Source: Authors.

Poland—EU

We start with the case of a RIA between a middle-income developing or transition economy and a large high-income country or bloc—such as with East European economies and the EU, or Mexico and the United States. On the political side, the most important element of likely gain comes from the policy lock-in argument. We saw in chapter 2 that two conditions need to be met for this argument to work; the country seeking lock-in must care about sanctions that the partner might impose, and the partner must have the incentive to impose sanctions, rather than let policy reversals go unremarked. Both these conditions seem likely to be met in this case. Suppose that "Poland" reneges on part of the agreement—perhaps imposing trade barriers, or violating political conditions. The partner (the "EU") is so large, and likely to account for such a high proportion of the country's trade that its actions will certainly impact on "Poland." At least when the countries are geographically close, the "EU" is likely to want to see economic and political stability in the region, and be prepared to act to enforce it. We have also scored "cooperation" positive; there is great potential for schemes ranging from environmental projects to technical assistance programs.

Turning to the economic arguments, there is considerable scope for gains from the "scale and competition" effects outlined in chapter 3. The middle-income country might typically have a broad range of industrial firms, many of them inefficient, perhaps because of lack of competition, or because they operate at small scale. Competition in a much larger market provides the opportunity for solving these problems.

What about the changes in trade flows and location? It seems likely that factor price differences should induce movement of relatively labor-intensive industrial activities to the middle-income country, in line with the experiences of Mexico, Hungary, and other parts of the European periphery we saw in chapter 3. Much of this might be driven by FDI, bringing with it new technology. A counter argument to this is that the established agglomeration of activity in the EU might draw activity out of the middle-income country, particularly since the EU is a "hub," benefiting from numerous bilateral "spoke" agreements. Whether or not this happens will depend on how closely the two regions are integrated. If barriers—including transport costs—are sufficiently low then the middle-income country is likely to be drawn into Europe-wide production networks. But if obstacles to trade or to FDI remain, the outcome may be less positive; the middle-income country might find its industry threatened by imports, yet not be a sufficiently attractive place for FDI inflows.

Finally, if the middle-income country retains high external tariffs, there is scope for it to suffer from trade diversion, although this is likely to be small insofar as affected sectors have low protection in the high-income country (with obvious exceptions, such as agriculture in the EU). Tariff revenue loss may be significant, since large volumes of trade are likely to be covered by an agreement of this sort.

Brazil—Argentina

Now consider a RIA between two middle-income countries, both perhaps of considerable size. We have marked in possible benefits under all the political headings.

On the economic side, a pair of countries at this stage of development offers perhaps the greatest potential for scale and competition effects. This might increase efficiency levels in domestic firms, attract FDI, and also lead to terms-of-trade improvements, as foreign suppliers react to the more competitive market. FDI might bring with it benefits of technology transfer. However, the usual question mark remains over these effects. Securing effective competition has often been obstructed, and achieving it requires investing in "deep integration"; policies to achieve this are discussed later in this chapter.

What about the relocation of industries between countries? If there are differences in comparative advantage or in market size and access, then integration will create forces for relocation. However, to the extent that the economies are similar, and already have established manufacturing sectors and the infrastructure that goes with it, it seems unlikely that this would be a one-way traffic. Some industries will expand in one country, others in the other, so there may be clustering of particular sectors rather than of activity as a whole, bringing gains from specialization rather than from the costs of divergence.

These are the benefits, but there are also likely costs. There is a danger of substantial trade diversion in such a RIA. The countries involved may have developed their industry behind protective barriers, meaning that production costs are well above world minima. If tariff preferences induce importers to switch the source of supply from the rest of the world to inefficient production in the partner country, this will reduce income. There will also be loss of government tariff revenue, its significance depending on initial tariff rates, on initial trade volumes, and on the ease with which governments are able to activate alternative fiscal instruments.

Burkina Faso—Côte d'Ivoire

Regional integration between two small low-income countries may offer some real opportunities for benefits from increased cooperation on economic projects—such as water management, or development of infrastructure, particularly between coastal and landlocked countries. As far as bargaining power goes, the main potential benefit is that of "being noticed," providing that the member countries are willing and able to take a concerted position on world issues. "Lock-in" effects are unlikely to be strong; they require both that the partner is itself committed to reform, and that it has political capital to invest in securing reform in the partner country.

Turning to economics, some sectors may benefit from scale and competition effects. Rationalization and removal of inefficient duplication of plants is a possible outcome, bringing with it efficiency gains. Market enlargement may also bring an FDI inflow. As usual, these potential gains can easily be frustrated, and it is also possible that even the combined market is too small for scale and competition effects to operate. Against these gains are the costs. If external tariffs remain high then trade diversion is likely. Related to this, inward-FDI may be "tariff jumping," in which case it is not necessarily beneficial. Both these effects will be associated with loss of tariff revenue, likely to be a major source of government revenue.

It is also in relatively closed South-South RIAs that we think that the scope for uneven internal development is greatest, with production concentrating in a few locations. If one region has a head start in manufacturing—due perhaps to its location, endowment of factors of production, or simply due to history—then this region may well expand at the expense of other regions ("Cote d'Ivoire" in table 4.1). Linkages are likely to be strong, because of the paucity of the business infrastructure, and manufacturing as a whole is sufficiently small that it will not run up against the "centrifugal" forces outlined in chapter 3. In this case then, the effects of the RIA will be very different across the members; beneficial for some, but possibly adverse for others.

Kenya—EU

Kenya—EU represents a RIA between a small low-income country and a large industrial country or bloc. In table 4.1 we have set effects on the EU at zero—simply reflecting the relative magnitudes of the countries.

What of the effects on the low-income partner? On the political side, we have scored the bargaining and being noticed rows at zero. In the domains of security, cooperation and policy lock-in there are potential gains. Once again, for a regional agreement to work as a commitment mechanism we look for two conditions to be satisfied. The first is that the country seeking lock-in must care about sanctions that the partner might impose. This condition seems likely to be met: If the partner is large, constituting a significant market for exports, and perhaps also a considerable source of aid and technical assistance the threat of sanctions will be powerful. The second condition is that the partner must have the incentive to impose sanctions, rather than let policy reversals go without response. This is more questionable. The "EU" is unlikely to be directly affected by policy reversal or even instability in a small remote developing country, but there may nevertheless be reasons for it to enforce an agreement. One might be a history of involvement with the region. Another is the reputation of the "EU" itself; if it has entered many such RIAs, then the effectiveness of all of them can be damaged by the failure of one.

Evidently, large question marks surround the willingness of our hypothetical industrial country to constitute an effective commitment mechanism. This is an argument for designing the agreement in a way that makes explicit the commitments to reform, and perhaps also the sanctions that are to be followed in the event of policy reversal.

Turning to the economics, there are three dominant issues. The first is trade diversion: Is a RIA with the "EU" likely to cause the source of imports to switch from other lower-cost suppliers to relatively high-cost "EU" production? This effect is likely to be small, insofar as the "EU" itself has low protection, so production costs are close to world minima. Transport costs could however be important if our hypothetical low-income country were much farther away from the "EU" than from other sources of supply of manufactures. The second issue is government revenue. There may be significant loss of tariff revenue, and the low-income country should look to the agreement to make this up.

Third, and perhaps most importantly, are the trade and location issues. Will such an agreement enable a low-income country to develop effective export activities, supplying the partner country? Is there a realistic likelihood that the low-income country can be drawn into a "production network," undertaking labor-intensive stages of production activity? Low-wage costs suggest so, but working against this are transport costs, quality of infrastructure, and security of market access. The potential advantage of a regional agreement is that it can make progress on reducing these obstacles. This suggests a need for such an agreement to be relatively deep, so it can overcome trade frictions and secure guaranteed market access, for example, by removing contingent protection.

Size and Multiple Membership: How Many?

Many countries are members of more than one RIA. Probably the most extreme example of this is the EU, in which each member is also a member of EU agreements with EFTA countries (the European Economic Area agreements), most Mediterranean countries (the Euro-Med agreements), and with East European countries (the Europe Agreements). A structure of this type has been termed "hub and spoke regionalism"; it places Europe at the hub of agreements with other countries, most of which are not linked to each other through RIAs.

Complex patterns of multiple membership appear elsewhere. In addition to the large Latin American RIAs, many Latin American countries also have bilateral agreements with other countries or groupings. For example, Chile is party to 11 trade agreements (APEC and the Latin American Integration Association, plus bilateral links with Argentina, Bolivia, Canada, Colombia, Ecuador, MERCOSUR, Mexico, Peru, and Venezuela). Panama is a member of nine trade agreements; Mexico of eight; Bolivia, Costa Rica, and Nicaragua of five; and El Salvador, Guatemala, and Honduras four each. The picture is equally complex for Eastern Europe, with the Slovak Republic belonging to nine RIAs; the Czech Republic and Slovenia belonging to eight; Estonia to six; and Hungary, Latvia, Poland, and Romania to five. The pattern of RIA memberships in East and southern Africa is given in figure 4.2, which reveals a pattern of overlapping memberships.

Figure 4.2 Regional Organizations in Southern and Eastern Africa

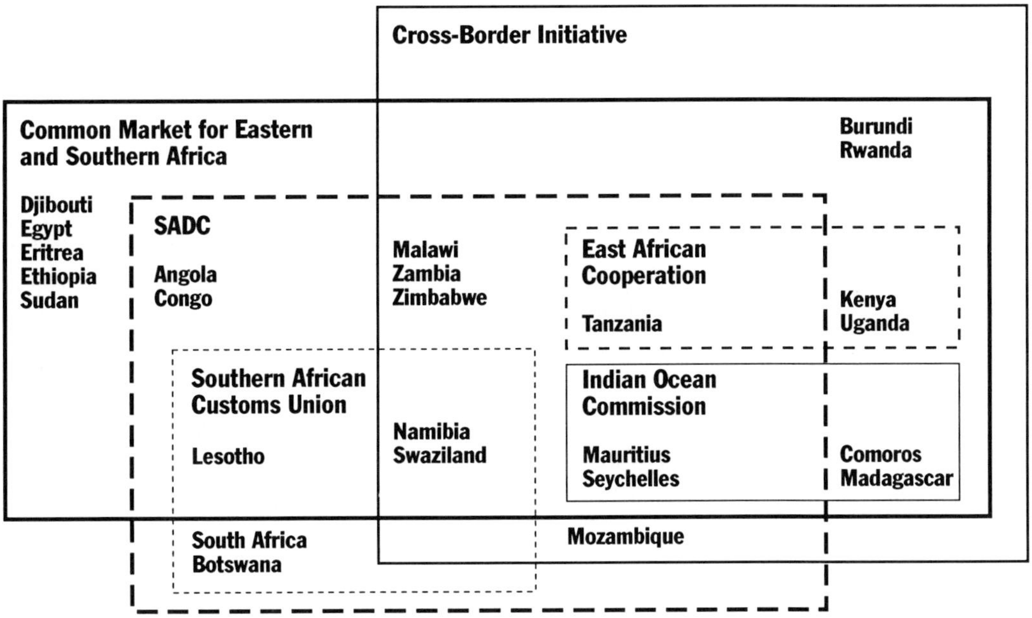

Source: Authors.

71

In some cases membership in multiple RIAs creates obligations made in one that contradict those made in others. Customs union members must all set the same external tariffs, yet Bolivia, Colombia, Ecudor, the Republica Boliviarana de Venezuela, and Peru form the Andean pact (a customs union), while Colombia and the Republica Boliviarana de Venezuela are also in the Group of 3, a free trade area with Mexico. Similarly (see figure 4.2), Lesotho, Namibia, and Swaziland belong to the Common Market for Eastern and Southern Africa while also belonging to Southern African Customs Union (SACU), a customs union with Botswana and South Africa. Tanzania belongs to SADC while being a member of the East African Cooperation, a customs union with Kenya and Uganda. These obligations are contradictory, so it may be unclear which will prevail in practice, and special conditions and exclusions may have to be formulated.

What are the benefits and costs of being in multiple RIAs? First, there are circumstances where gains can be derived, by some countries at least, from being in more than one RIA. The best example of this is being the hub of "hub and spoke" regionalism. If one country (or group of countries) has RIAs with a number of countries that maintain barriers between each other, this hub country becomes the preferred location for investment—firms can reach more markets tariff-free than they can from any of the other locations—and this will tend to bid up factor prices and raise real income in the hub.

Second, membership in multiple RIAs may lead to complexity, which can hinder private sector decisionmaking. The extent to which this happens depends on how complex the individual RIAs are. Membership in a number of relatively loose free trade areas may be straightforward, but even here there is a possibility for conflicting rules—for example, rules of origin requirements—that are nontransparent and complicate the business environment. At worst, there are inconsistencies (as when some customs union members are also in a free trade area), which can only create uncertainty about how the inconsistency is to be resolved, and is thus likely to dampen investment.

Third, securing the full gains from a RIA may require considerable government commitment—for example, tackling the difficult issues of deep and wide integration—and membership of many RIAs may be a diversion from this.

These points are relevant considerations not only for a government considering membership of multiple RIAs, but also for incumbent members deciding on accession of additional countries. There is, in most cases, a tradeoff between the depth of integration that can be achieved and the size of the RIA. (This tradeoff has been evident in the different positions taken by EU member states in discussion of enlargement of the EU). The tradeoff can be shifted by requiring that new members accept the entire package of policies implemented by existing members (the *acquis communitaire* in EU parlance). While this may make it easier for incumbents to accept new members, it may reduce the desirability of membership for these new countries. In general then, we expect early members to have more say in setting the rules—and therefore receive larger benefits—than later members.

4.2 External Trade Policy: How Much Preference?

A FUNDAMENTAL ISSUE CONFRONTING ANY GOVERNMENT considering a regional integration agreement is the external trade policy that will prevail. There are two dimensions to this issue: first, the level of external protection that will apply after the agreement is made, and second, whether to set this external trade policy in a concerted manner.

Openness to the Outside World

Some of the costs and benefits of RIA membership depend directly on the external trade policy stance. This creates strong arguments for pursuing a policy of external openness in conjunction with regional integration.

First, trade diversion is both more likely—and more costly should it occur—the higher the external trade barriers. It is more likely, since the relative price differences created by preferential liberalization will be greater with a higher external tariff, inducing trade diversion in more sectors. It is also more costly, since a higher external tariff will provide greater incentives for inefficient sectors to expand. Producers are able to charge high prices (because the tariff protects them from world competition) and capture what was previously tariff revenue on internal trade. Fundamentally, the gains from competition with low-cost suppliers—gains to consumers, gains in developing an efficient industrial structure, and competition-induced efficiency gains at the firm level—may be forgone if competition from the lowest cost suppliers is inhibited. These are arguments both for low tariffs on average, and for tariff schedules that are relatively uniform, avoiding peaks. Very high rates in particular sectors are almost certain to produce diversion—such as in EU agriculture.

A further argument for low external tariffs relates to the likelihood of agglomeration occurring, and the RIA consequently causing divergence of economic structure. We argued in chapter 3 that one of the forces driving agglomeration is linkages between firms—the dependence of firms on other local firms for supplies, and on local firms and markets for their sales. The more closed is the RIA, the more inward-oriented will be its firms, increasing the strength of local linkages and making it more likely that the RIA will develop a monocentric economic structure. Research by Ades and Glaeser (1995) examined 85 countries, and showed that the population of the largest city is greater the higher are tariff barriers and the lower the share of imports in GNP. Krugman and Hanson (1993) have documented how Mexico's opening to trade (largely with the United States) brought a deconcentration of manufacturing from the congested Mexico City region.[1]

A counter argument to external openness might be that the RIA liberalization brings with it adjustment costs, and simultaneous external liberalization magnifies these to an unacceptable level. The problem with this argument is that adjustment costs are only worth paying, for an adjustment in the right direction. High-tariff peaks might induce costly economic changes that are moves away from economic efficiency. Simulation studies of regional integration involving developing countries and large, high-income nations or blocs (such as the EU) suggest that the adjustment costs associated with RIA implementation are as high as those that would arise if trade liberalization were implemented on a nondiscriminatory basis (Rutherford, Rutström, and Tarr 1999).

Customs Union or Free Trade Area?

In a free trade area (FTA), countries are free to set their own external trade policy, whereas in a customs union (CU) the RIA as a whole sets a common external policy. Of the 162 RIAs notified to the GATT/WTO by August 1998, 143 were FTAs and 19 were CUs.[2] A CU typically requires greater political commitment, because countries have to agree to a common external policy and set up budgetary mechanisms to distribute the tariff revenue between member countries. A central issue for countries planning to integrate their trade is whether to choose an FTA or CU.

The great advantage of a CU is that, because members have a common external tariff, it is possible to have much simpler internal border formalities—and possibly none at all. In contrast, an FTA leaves external trade policy to individual member governments, and faces a problem known as *trade deflection;* the redirection of imports from outside countries through the FTA member with the lowest external tariff, to exploit the tariff differential. If unconstrained, this reduces the effective tariff of every member to that of the lowest plus the transportation cost involved in indirect importing (which is a wasted real resource cost). The usual solution is *rules of origin*—the apparently reasonable requirement that goods qualifying for tariff-free trade should be produced in a member country, rather than just passing through it.

In practice, the costs of implementing rules of origin are high. They mean that controls on goods crossing internal frontiers have to be retained to ensure compliance and to collect customs duties that are due. Some years ago these costs were estimated at 3 to 5 percent of f.o.b. prices for EFTA-European Community trade (Herin 1986). They also allow customs authorities—and individual customs officers—a good deal of discretion, and the attendant danger that such discretion might be abused.

Rules of origin are particularly complex because they have to take into account tariffs on imported intermediate goods used in products manufactured within the FTA. The principle behind a rule of origin is that imports from outside the FTA should pay the tariff of the country of final sale, but additional value added in FTA members should be tariff-free. For example, if one million dollars worth of shirts are manufactured in FTA member A and exported to member B, and these shirts use $100k of cotton imported from outside the FTA on which the country B tariff is 20 percent, then $20k of duty is payable to B; furthermore, the exporting firm should be rebated any tariff it paid to country A on the cotton. In practice calculations are not made on such an exact basis but instead according to more or less arbitrary rules, typically stating that exports have to derive a certain proportion of their value from local content or undergo certain production processes within the FTA to obtain duty-free treatment.

The rules are complex and hard to negotiate (the EU's agreement with Poland has 81 pages of small print in its rules of origin section, and NAFTA some 200 [Krueger 1997]). Since they do not match the exact inputs in each commodity, they introduce further biases and sources of distortion. For example, NAFTA rules of origin in some sectors have serious protective effects that shift trade and investment patterns from lower- to higher-cost sources. Most clothing produced in Mexico gains tariff-free access to the North American U.S. and Canadian markets only if its inputs are virtually 100 percent sourced in North America (WTO 1995). In the automobile industry, the origin requirement of 62.5 percent local content has induced Japanese automobile manufacturers with plants in Canada to produce components in the United States rather than import cheaper ones from Japan. NAFTA rules of origin require color television tubes to be of North American origin, causing five television tube factories to be planned or established in North America by Japanese or the Republic of Korean firms, probably at the expense of expansion in Southeast Asia.

It is also worth noting that even with complex rules of origin in place, the problem of imports to the FTA entering through the country with the lowest external tariff is not entirely solved. A low-tariff partner can meet its own requirements for a product from the rest of the world, and export a corresponding amount (or all) of its own production to its partners. This is *indirect trade deflection* (Robson 1998).

Thus, there are substantial benefits to going to a CU, yet, as we saw above, only a small minority of RIAs notified to the GATT/WTO are in fact CUs. What are the costs?

First, harmonization of external trade policy means a loss of national autonomy. Second, we saw in chapter 2 the potential for politically divisive redistributions due to a common external tariff—for example, in the antebellum United States. Political institutions need to be put in place to ensure that these tariffs are set in a consensual way. Furthermore, tariff revenues generated by the common external tariff have to be distributed between member countries, and this too can be divisive. In the EU these revenues are part of the central budget and are spent on agreed programs, yet the level of each member's net contribution or receipt from the budget remains contentious. In many developing country customs unions, difficulties of agreeing on a common external tariff and distribution of revenues have proven to be great. Thus, the GCC has to date not been able to achieve consensus on its common external tariff. Similarly, the implementation of a common external tariff by CARICOM, originally scheduled for 1981, was delayed until the 1990s; the original scheme, adopted in 1991, was subsequently revised, and

CARICOM members are in the process of implementing a new tariff structure (IDB 1998). In the case of the CACM, the common external tariff was rendered largely ineffective because of exemptions granted by some members for "necessary" imports (De la Torre and Kelley 1992).

The third problem with a common external trade policy is the additional adjustment costs—and lobby opposition—that may be encountered in moving to the common schedule. A good example is the difficulty that the EU had in harmonizing nontariff barriers. Despite being a customs union, for its first 30 years the EU allowed members to maintain their own quotas on certain third country imports (for instance, clothing, footwear, and steel) and prevented those goods from crossing internal borders (Winters 1992, 1993).

These three costs of forming a CU are minimized of member countries are more similar to each other, as in South-South RIAs rather than North-South RIAs. Schiff (2000) shows that the ratio of FTAs to CUs is 6 to 20 times higher for North-South RIAs then for South-South ones.

CUs, FTAs, and the External Tariff

There is a potentially important interaction between our first point—the desirability of open external trade—and the choice between an FTA and a CU, because FTAs and CUs create different incentives for setting external tariffs.

Several arguments suggest that an FTA may create downward pressure on external tariffs. First, trade diversion may become apparent; if a country sees itself importing a good from a partner country at a higher cost than similar goods from nonmembers, this may induce it to cut tariffs on these external imports. Second, if there is trade deflection, high-tariff countries lose tariff revenue, as imports come in through low tariff countries. This creates an incentive to cut tariffs to just below the level of their partners, and thereby capture the tariff revenue. Third, if duties on inputs used to make exports to other members cannot be rebated, high import tariffs render final goods uncompetitive to exporters. This concern was apparently behind Canada's decision to reduce 1,500 tariffs on inputs in 1995, shortly after NAFTA started.

The situation in CUs is quite different. Creating a customs union provides an (unavoidable!) opportunity to review the tariff structures and create new institutions for determining trade policy. National tariffs must be harmonized at some agreed level, and in the process, international obligations—notably those to the WTO—must be respected. Unfortunately, most of the arguments about the incentives for tariff setting in a CU do not lean toward external openness.

The first argument is that, by coordinating their trade policies, CU members may have a market power that individual countries lack. Import tariffs can improve a country's terms of trade, since by cutting the volume imported they reduce the world price of the product. This effect is going to be larger, the larger the country or bloc imposing the tariff. Furthermore, countries in a RIA may be able to increase their negotiating power against the rest of the world. If they are able to negotiate effectively as a bloc (which does not always happen) this additional power will change the outcome of trade negotiations. A related argument is that, in trade negotiations, a CU may be able to gain disproportionate power over certain issues by letting a particular member "lead" negotiations. If a more aggressive member leads negotiations with the rest of the world on an issue, the union may be able to extract a more favorable deal because threats to retaliate (with the whole of the union's resources) will be more credible.[3] Whether this leads to lower protection overall depends on whether a more aggressive union can achieve a more liberal outcome by virtue of its readiness to retaliate, or whether it actually needs to use its retaliatory muscle.

The internal process of decisionmaking within the CU may also place an upward pressure on tariffs. Consider a situation in which each member country has an interest in raising protection in one sector and reducing it in all others, and each country has a veto over reductions in protection. Unless there is effective intra-CU negotiation, this creates the possibility of a classic "prisoners' dilemma" outcome with high protection in all sectors, even though each country would be better off with low protection in all sectors. Although it might be hoped that negotiation within a CU could avoid prisoners' dilemmas, there are enough examples from the EU to not engender optimism. The EU allows countries disproportionate influence over policy—up to (and including) veto power—in areas in which they claim "vital interests." Winters (1994) shows that the prisoners' dilemma outcome is quite likely to arise in small groups of decisionmakers, and experience suggests the same outcome. Indeed, the unanimity with which trade policy decisions pass (in 1995 the EU Council of Ministers passed 92 of its 94 common trade policy decisions unanimously) suggests that countries were willing to acquiesce to perceived "vital interests" of particular members (Bilal 1998).

The CU will also change the power of lobbies. It is possible that lobbying pressure within a CU may be diluted, compared with national lobbying for protection within an FTA. There may be more opposition to overcome (Panagariya and Findlay 1994; de Melo, Panagariya, and Rodrik 1993) or more representatives to influence (Richardson 1994). Other arguments cut in the other direction. For example, each country might find that initially its industry and agriculture more or less cancelled each other out, but if integration lets agriculture lobbies cooperate (because they produce the same things) while the industry lobbies compete (because they produce different things) the CU may end up with agricultural protection. It is worth noting that there is a massive lobbying industry in Brussels, where the number of lobbying organizations grew from 300 in 1970 to some 3,000 in 1990. Expenditure on lobbying was estimated at $150 million in 1990, and increased rapidly. By 1998, there were 13,000 professional lobbyists in Brussels, approaching one for every European Commission staff member (*The Economist*, August 14, 1998).

4.3 How Deep?

THERE IS A LARGE MENU OF CHOICES CONCERNING THE DEPTH of integration that can be sought in a RIA. We argued in chapter 3 that the gains from competition and scale effects might not be achieved unless other policies causing segmentation of markets were removed, and firms in different countries were induced to compete head-on. Simple removal of tariffs while other obstacles remain in place may not be sufficient to achieve this. However, removing these obstacles is not without cost. For example, a CU is "deeper" than an FTA (it avoids the border costs associated with enforcement of rules of origin), but it brings with it other complexities related to choosing the common external tariff and distributing the revenue. In this section we look in detail at other policy measures that can be adopted to try and secure greater market integration.

Contingent Protection

Many RIAs retain contingent protection—restrictions on intrabloc trade that are applied in a more or less well-defined set of circumstances.

These include antidumping, countervailing duties (in response to foreign subsidies), and "emergency protection" to address balance of payments problems or to protect an industry from surges in imports. While contingent protection has been abolished within the EU, it remains applicable in all the EU's agreements with other countries except the European Economic Area. Within some RIAs contingent protection is widely used; in MERCOSUR, Argentina initiated 33 antidumping cases on imports from Brazil between 1992–96 (Tavares and Tineo 1998). Where these contingent protection measures have been left in place, countries recognize that they provide obstacles to trade, but have weighed the political and economic costs of their removal greater than the benefits. What are the benefits and costs of removing these measures, as has been done in the EU, the Canada-Chile FTA, and the Australia-New Zealand agreement?

Contingent protection provides a major barrier to trade, not only when actually applied to trade flows, but also by its mere existence, which has a "chilling" effect on trade. Just the surveillance of trade flows has been shown to have a negative impact on the volume of trade (Winters 1994). The threat of initiation of antidumping actions can lead to an immediate loss of markets for exporters, as importers seek to avoid the costs of posting the bonds required by customs authorities while the investigation is ongoing. Empirical estimates of the "chilling" effect on trade find that threatened exporters often agree to raise prices and maintain historical market shares, so contingent protection becomes an instrument facilitating collusion between domestic and foreign firms (Messerlin 1990; Staiger and Wolak 1989).

These are powerful arguments for abolition of contingent protection, but they encounter several counter-arguments. The first is that dumping can be predatory, when a foreign firm (or cartel) seeks to force domestic competitors out of the market by pricing below cost—with the intention of raising prices once the competition is gone. However, research suggests that predation is very much the exception, not the rule in antidumping cases, and that in over 90 percent of actual antidumping actions an antitrust authority would not have intervened on competition, let alone predation, grounds (Messerlin 1997; Schöne 1996). The consensus among most economists is that antidumping as it is practiced today has nothing to do with predation. Furthermore, if there is predation, national antitrust should be able to address the problem; and this can be done unilaterally—there is no need for international agreement or harmonizing competition regimes.

The second counter-argument is that if countervailing duties are to be suspended, then measures also need to be taken to restrain or coordinate industrial subsidies that may have a negative impact on domestic firms. When such subsidies are being used there are valid theoretical economic justifications for the use of countervailing duties (Dixit 1988). However, in general, contingent protection is an inefficient instrument to deal with the effects of foreign subsidies or industrial policies, because it imposes additional costs on domestic consumers without greatly increasing the incentives of the foreign government to change its policies. Small countries in particular are unlikely to have much success by pursuing retaliatory policies—all they will end up doing is adding an additional distortion to consumption. The appropriate policy is to draft rules that restrict the ability of RIA members to use industrial policies in ways that are detrimental to the welfare of other member countries. In practice, this may be difficult to achieve; only a limited number of RIAs have done much to discipline the ability of members to provide subsidies.

Finally, there may be strident opposition from lobby groups to the abolition of these measures. Antidumping cases are frequently initiated by producer lobbies, and these may be virulent opponents of their withdrawal. In practice the political power of these groups goes a long way toward explaining why contingent protection frequently remains in place in RIAs, despite the overall commitment to liberalize intrabloc trade flows. Continued access to such instruments may be required in order to "sell" the more general liberalization reform package.

Borders, Product Standards, and Red Tape

Trading across international borders encounters many real costs: delays, form-filling, recertification of products, and so on. Even if there are no duties, border formalities themselves create barriers and can be quite wasteful. For example, customs procedures can be duplicative or redundant, as when tax authorities in an exporting country require data similar to that demanded by the importer's customs officials—but in a different format. It has been estimated that border formalities on *intra*-EU trade in the early 1990s were equivalent to over 1.2 percent of the gross value of internally traded goods. The EU had already implemented procedures to cut these costs, and in many other RIAs the costs of border formalities are many times larger.[4]

81

Additional barriers to trade are created by variations in national product standards. Estimates from Egypt in the early 1990s, showed just how significant standards-related "red tape" in customs were; redundant testing and idiosyncratic standards alone imposed taxes equivalent to between 5 and 90 percent of the value of shipments (Hoekman and Konan 1999).

Barriers of this type prevent effective international competition. They provide opportunities for corruption. They are usually real resource costs—unlike tariffs, where revenue gets transferred to the government, the barriers use up administrative and technical time and effort. What can be done, within a RIA, to simplify them?

Border Formalities

Border formalities can be reduced by good customs administration and the use of standard practice on procedures. Much of this is possible independently of RIA membership, by adopting best practices in the area of customs administration and implementing the relevant international conventions aimed at trade facilitation. The World Customs Organization is the primary organization promoting the standardization and simplification of customs procedures around the world, in particular the Kyoto Convention of 1973, currently undergoing a major revision. Adopting the revised procedures has been argued to be the single most comprehensive prospect for true international trade facilitation (Staples 1998). Some of the needed measures are easier to implement within a RIA. One reason is simply the inherent simplicity of not collecting duties on internal trade. Another is that it may be easier to develop common approaches and institutions, such as the adoption of standard forms.

Product Standards

The issues raised by product standards are more complex, since countries can genuinely differ on what they regard as acceptable levels of standards. Countries seeking to reduce the barriers created by differing standards can follow two alternative routes—harmonization and mutual recognition.

The baseline principle governing treatment of imports in most trade agreements is "national treatment," which requires that governments treat foreign products or producers that enter their territory in the same way as domestic counterparts, in terms of internal taxes, health and safety standards, competition rules, and so on. The principle has always been a basic building block of international trade treaties, and ensures that liberalization commitments cannot be circumvented by discriminatory application of domestic policies—such as an excise tax that is higher for foreign than for domestic products. While national treatment is a powerful source of discipline on RIA members, problems arise if national product standards differ, requiring the sort of expensive retesting we saw above.[5]

These issues are nothing new. In the past they have often been resolved by harmonization around international standards. Between 1860 and 1914 more than 30 intergovernmental organizations emerged to harmonize product standards, particularly on infrastructure: for example, mail (1863), marine signaling (1864), technical railway standards (1883), ocean telegraphy (1897), and aerial navigation (1910) (Murphy 1994). International interconnection norms, agreed under auspices of the International Telecommunications Union, eliminated the need for telegrams to be printed at each border post, walked across, and retyped. The Radiotelegraph Union aimed to prevent a global radio monopoly by requiring interconnection across different technologies. Intergovernmental organizations proliferated after World War II, including such standards-setting bodies as the International Maritime Organization, the World Customs Organization, and the Bank for International Settlements. However, these bodies do not cover the great bulk of products that make up most of world trade.[6]

An alternative is to harmonize by unilaterally adopting the standards of another country or group of countries. In 1992 Canada adopted U.S. auto emission standards to ensure that its automakers could realize economies of scale by avoiding separate production lines for their home and U.S. markets. Switzerland, similarly, adopted the EU regime on technical regulations and industrial standards so Swiss goods can enter and circulate in the EU on the same basis as EU-produced goods (Messerlin 1998). Many developing countries use legal regimes developed in Europe or the United States, usually by maintaining systems inherited from a colonial past or military occupation. Others have deliberately adopted foreign norms. South Korea imported many West German and U.S. product standards in the 1950s as part of a strategy to upgrade the quality of industrial production and foster exports.

Despite these possibilities, most countries still maintain their own distinct product standards. Attempts to harmonize within a RIA require developing a set of RIA-specific common standards, set either by intergovernmental cooperation or by the cession of sovereignty to common or supranational institutions. In the EU, the European Commission has been delegated the power of proposing directives and regulations and the Court of Justice given the task of enforcement. EU experience suggests that this process is extremely slow and painful. Early efforts toward harmonization centered on food standards—the first "harmonization directive" issued in 1962 dealt with food coloring—and progress was very slow, in part because adoption of a Community-wide norm required unanimity. It took over a decade to reach agreement on the composition of fruit jams and mineral water, and only nine directives on foodstuffs were adopted between 1962 and 1979. Differences in national norms, reflecting national tastes, history, legal regimes—and producer lobbies seeking to restrict competition from imports—made it difficult to achieve the required consensus. For example, Germans set great store by their *Reinheitsgebot,* a standard established in 1516 specifying that beer may have only four ingredients (malted barley, hops, yeast, water). Other countries include preservatives or additives.

If harmonization is not pursued, the alternative route to settling standards issues is "mutual recognition," under which member countries simply accept that goods that are legally introduced into circulation in one member state cannot be barred from entering and being sold in another. This principle was incorporated into the Single Market program and has proved to be a powerful tool for increasing cross-border competition in European markets.[7]

However, mutual recognition raises two quite difficult issues. First, countries have to be able to agree on the minimum norms that should be met to safeguard public health and safety or maintain the integrity of public networks. Second, there has to be mutual trust in the competence and ability of the national institutions responsible for enforcing the relevant mandatory standards. Thus, even if all members accept the levels at which standards are set, it may require significant institutional strengthening for one country to accept that another's testing and certification procedures are adequate. One way of addressing this constraint is to rely on third party conformity assessment of goods and services, and seek agreement that certification by such specialized entities will be accepted by all members of a RIA. To date, however, this has been an option that has not been pursued vigorously in RIAs.

Discrimination in Public Procurement

If RIA membership is to secure effective competition, then competition should extend to government procurement—an area that often accounts for as much as 10 percent of GDP. Yet, in practice, governments frequently permit or require public entities to discriminate in favor of domestic firms when procuring goods and services. This can take the form of price preferences, local content rules, or residency requirements.

Progress in eliminating discrimination in public procurement can, in principle, be made independently of RIA membership, by consistent application of the national treatment principle and procedures outlined in the WTO Agreement on Government Procurement. In practice, progress at the multilateral level has been slow—virtually no developing countries have signed the voluntary WTO agreement (Hoekman and Mavroidis 1997). RIAs offer a potential avenue to make more rapid progress. However, only a limited number of RIAs have included liberalization of public procurement as an objective or made progress in forcing government entities to abide by the national treatment principle (EU, NAFTA). Progress in this area has proven to be difficult to achieve. A recent evaluation of the pattern of purchasing by European government entities found that public sector import penetration increased from an estimated 6 percent in 1987 to some 10 percent in 1994 (Gordon, Rimmer, and Arrowsmith 1998). Thus, on average, 90 percent of all purchases in the EU continue to be sourced from national firms, despite vigorous efforts by the EC Commission to eliminate discriminatory procurement practices.

4.4 How Wide?

POLICYMAKERS ALSO FACE CHOICES OVER THE RANGE OF activities to integrate. The discussion so far has focused on merchandise trade and integration of goods markets, but there are other aspects of cross-border economic interaction that may remain tightly regulated. The main examples concern trade in factors of production and trade in services. What are the costs and benefits of extending liberalization to these other cross-border interactions?

Investment Flows

At various points we have referred to the likely effects of FDI flows in a RIA. These may be flows from outside, or from partners within the RIA, as plants move to exploit the comparative advantage of different locations and to compete more directly with host country firms. In practice, there can be substantial barriers to such investment.[8] The barriers take many forms, including: absolute barriers to establishment in some sectors or activities; requirements that foreign equity not exceed a certain percentage of the total; domestic content requirements or export requirements, requirements that FDI projects meet targets not imposed on national firms; and obstacles to repatriation of profits.

Little progress has been made on liberalizing these restrictions on a multilateral basis. The OECD's proposed Multilateral Agreement on Investment sought to overcome some of these barriers, but agreement could not be reached. A WTO working group is studying the desirability of multilateral investment rules, but there are strong differences of opinion regarding the costs and benefits of a multilateral set of disciplines in this area. Within RIAs too, progress has often been slow, although individual member states of many RIAs have been unilaterally liberalizing FDI regimes. Argentina and Brazil still restrict FDI flows in a number of sectors, independent of whether or not the potential investor originates in MERCOSUR; CARICOM has only liberalized investment in banking; the CACM countries do not have a common investment regime. But many RIAs do include provisions to liberalize investment flows: such as NAFTA, the Group of Three, GCC, and SACU.

The case for liberalizing investment is strong. As we have seen at many points above, FDI is an important route through which developing countries can benefit from RIA membership. Agreeing to apply national treatment and the right of establishment for investors helps ensure that production choices are not distorted, and is important for governments seeking to use RIAs as "lock-in" or commitment devices. Leaving FDI off the table sends a strong signal to the international financial community that a government may wish to continue to restrict international transactions.

Services Liberalization

Service trade is inherently more complex than goods trade, for two reasons. First, in many service activities problems of asymmetric information are particularly acute; the purchaser does not know the quality of a professional service being purchased until after it has been paid for and consumed. And second, service trade frequently requires consumers and providers to be at the same place at the same time.

The first of these complexities creates a proper need for regulation of such service activities. Service suppliers must obtain certification or licensing in such fields as financial services, law, accountancy, and medicine. However, standards are often set by professional bodies that have an interest not only in creating a reputation for ensuring quality, but also in restricting entry and limiting competition. The second complexity—that services providers typically have to be established in the country they are supplying—is an inherent obstacle to international trade.

The combination of these two considerations has made services trade notoriously prone to trade restrictions, and hard to liberalize. We see existing services trade restrictions taking many forms. Many countries restrict the access of foreign services and service suppliers to domestic markets, and sometimes trade in services is simply prohibited.[9] Rights of supply may be restricted to domestic firms (such as in domestic transportation and basic telecommunication services), or to domestic residents (such as in legal, insurance, educational, surveying, or investment advisory services). Even if there are no formal prohibitions, there are often major barriers to entry. Professional standards are set in a way that requires foreigners to engage in costly recertification. Rights of access to telecommunications networks are often restricted: for example, where a dominant telecommunication carrier—public or private—imposes restrictions on the ability of new service providers to link to the network, or forces them to build infrastructure to reach interconnection points. Discrimination in ancillary services—not being listed in computer reservation systems—can substantially reduce the competitiveness of an airline. Limitations on advertising are a common way to limit the ability of foreign insurance firms to compete, and distribution arrangements can effectively bar market access for branded products.

This restrictive starting point, and the fact that most of the barriers are essentially quantity restrictions (prohibitions and regulations rather than tariffs) means that gains from opening up services trade to international competition are likely to be particularly large.[10] Indeed, from a starting point of prohibitive barriers, a preferential liberalization cannot be "trade diverting," so a major source of ambiguity about gains from preferential liberalization is absent. Furthermore, there will be no loss of tariff revenue for government, since rents created by the regulatory obstacles are typically collected by protected firms and workers. This does, of course, raise its own political economy difficulties in seeing through a liberalization.

In addition, the fact that the service sector is an input to so many other activities in the economy—production, commerce, trade, and education—makes it particularly important that the sector function efficiently. For example, the fact that services are an input to production means that failure to liberalize them faces local producers with higher costs than necessary, at a time when the RIA is possibly increasing competition and reducing the price of their output. This can give rise to the phenomenon of negative effective protection; output is not receiving tariff protection, but inputs are (implicitly, in the form of the barriers to service trade), so creating negative incentives for the development of activities that use these services. Estimates for Egypt suggest that trade barriers in services reduced effective rates of protection for manufacturing activities by some 30 percentage points (Djankov and Hoekman 1997). Since services are an input to trade, service sector inefficiencies can be damaging for many sectors of the economy. Agricultural output can be lost due to poor transportation and storage facilities, and substandard communication networks can raise the costs of doing business. Recent studies of Egypt drew attention to the fact maritime shipping was a monopoly—and fees were 25 percent higher than those in neighboring countries for equivalent routes. Fees charged by the public companies providing port services for handling and storage of goods were 30 percent higher (Mohieldin 1997). It has been estimated that a service liberalization that reduces average services prices by 15 percent could lead to estimated welfare gains for Egypt of some 5 to 10 percent of GDP (Hoekman and Konan 1999).

Most RIAs have not gone much beyond what was achieved in the General Agreement on Trade in Services (GATS). The main exceptions are the EU and NAFTA, although in all cases effective liberalization of services was not initiated until the 1990s. NAFTA has made substantial progress using a negative list system, so all service sectors are covered unless specifically exempted.[11] Other RIAs vary in their coverage of services. The Group of Three is similar to NAFTA, although sectoral coverage is narrower. In MERCOSUR, free circulation of services is a long-term objective to be achieved by 2007; progress has been slow, with members still negotiating a framework agreement. ASEAN members have agreed to full liberalization (on a preferential basis) in most services by 2020. The FTAs between the EU and Mediterranean countries do not include services, while those with the Central and Eastern European countries do. ANDEAN, CACM, and SADC have so far made little progress (Hoekman and Sauvé 1994; Page 1997).

If liberalization is to be pursued, it can proceed through various channels. GATS was negotiated at the WTO as part of the Uruguay Round, and WTO members have agreed to begin a new round of negotiations on services in the year 2000. This provides an opportunity to improve the structure of the rules and to achieve a higher level of liberalization commitments.

There are several reasons to think that RIAs may, for many countries, offer a more effective route to service liberalization. First, service liberalization may involve labor mobility—service providers need to become established locally, and this typically involves temporary if not permanent residence. Politically, this may be easier to achieve in a RIA than on a nondiscriminatory basis. Second, procedures are needed to make sure that quality standards are met. These issues are conceptually similar to those we saw with product standards—agreement on harmonization or, if mutually agreeable standards are in place, on mutual recognition. Achieving these within a RIA may be easier than establishing them for all comers.

However, service liberalization within a RIA is not something that is likely to be achieved easily. The very fact that these sectors are highly protected by nontariff instruments means that there are substantial vested interests, and considerable political effort will be needed to overcome them. Many RIAs have found it difficult to make much progress, and only now is the EU effectively securing market opening in these areas.

Further Areas

Investment and services are the two most important areas, beyond merchandise trade, where there are gains from widening the scope of integration. Of course, the scope can be set wider still—to include labor mobility, fiscal harmonization, and monetary union. We end this chapter by cautioning that extending the scope too broadly may detract from the economic benefits of integration. Some of the benefits from trade that arise out of differences between countries and the attempts to iron these out—by, for example, RIA-wide minimum wage legislation—will inhibit the very mechanisms by which countries can gain from integration.

4.5 Conclusion

ONE REASONABLY FIRM CONCLUSION IS THAT FOR MOST developing countries, and especially for the poorer ones, a North-South RIA with a large industrial country is likely to be superior to a South-South RIA with a developing country. The reasons are that:

- South-South RIAs are more likely to generate divergence, with the less developed member losing relative to the more developed one.
- South-South RIAs are more likely to generate trade diversion.
- North-South RIAs are more likely to generate useful transfers of technology.
- North-South RIAs are more likely to provide lock-in mechanisms in the area of politics (such as democracy) and economics (in terms of policy credibility).
- Given the industrial partner's superior institutions, a North-South RIA may provide more benefits from "deep integration" than a South-South RIA.
- Given a larger endowment difference between member countries in a North-South RIA than in a South-South one, a developing country may be able to better exploit its comparative advantage in a North-South RIA.
- The developing country partner is unlikely to capture most of the above-mentioned benefits of North-South integration unless it undertakes economic reforms.
- Though this chapter advocates forming or joining a RIA with a industrial country or region, whether and under what circumstances the latter will allow the developing country to join is unclear. This is examined in chapter 5.

Other conclusions include:

- For any RIA, lowering external trade barriers (up to the optimum level) is beneficial: it will increase the RIA's gains or reduce its losses.

- Though there are substantial benefits from a CU compared with an FTA in terms of simplicity of intrabloc trade regulations there are also costs in terms of loss of sovereignty, difficulty in setting the common external tariff and sharing the tariff revenues. Thus, most recent RIAs have been FTAs, and mostly North-South ones where these costs of forming a CU are likely to be high.

- For middle-income countries—such as the members of MERCOSUR or ASEAN—there may be sufficient gains from scale and competition effects to justify a RIA between them, but fully capturing these effects will require "deep integration" measures, and expansion and contraction of sectors and firms decided by the market.

- However, if a middle-income country is located close to a large industrial RIA—such as Mexico, and Eastern European and Mediterranean countries—then it is likely to best capture the benefits of enhanced scale and competition by joining that RIA.

Notes

1. For development of this argument see Fujita, Krugman, and Venables (1999) and Venables (1999).

2. Source: WTO. Of course, many RIAs contain other elements as well; this classification refers only to their policies on trade in goods.

3. Gatsios and Karp (1991, 1995).

4. In 1988 the EU had already adopted a Single Administrative Document and many members had simplified procedures to reduce customs burdens for large traders. The average customs clearance transaction in developing countries involves 25 to 30 different parties, 40 documents, 200 data elements, some 30 of which are requested at least 30 times, and 60 to 70 percent of which must be re-keyed at least once (Roy 1998).

5. Article 36 of the Treaty of Rome permits EU members to maintain domestic policies that restrict trade if this is needed to protect national health, security, morals, or the environment. Virtually all RIAs have similar provisions.

6. Neither do they usually include enforcement mechanisms. Resolving interstate conflicts has always figured on the agenda of international conferences and organizations, but has often been ineffective. Early in this century a number of proposals were made to develop international instruments to extend binding arbitration to intellectual property, the principle of equality of foreigners in taxation (national treatment), civil and commercial procedure, customs tariffs, the right of foreigners to hold property, the regulation of companies, and claims for damages. These were opposed by countries that sought to retain their national sovereignty (Murphy 1994). Most of the bodies mentioned earlier (except for the WTO) do not have binding dispute settlement mechanisms.

7. It originates from a landmark 1979 case, in which the European Court of Justice found that a German ban on the sale of a French Cassis de Dijon used to prepare an aperitif, kir, could not be justified on the basis of public safety or health. At the same time, procedures for harmonization were simplified by shifting to a majority voting rule for standards harmonization (Neven 1996). During 1986–97 some 250 harmonization directives were adopted

in the EU under majority voting rules, compared to a total of only 225 between 1958 and 1985, when the unanimity principle applied (Messerlin 1998).

8.   We look only at long-term investment, not at the issue of regulation of short-run capital flows.

9.   What follows draws on Hoekman and Braga (1997).

10. Typically a doubling of protective barriers more than doubles the real income cost of the barrier.

11. For example, a NAFTA Professional Services Annex sets out procedures for developing standards of professional practice, requires the abolition of citizenship and permanent residency requirements in licensing and certifying professional service providers, and establishes work programs to liberalize licensing for foreign legal consultants and engineers.

CHAPTER 5

Trade Blocs and the World Trading System

Introduction

DOES REGIONAL INTEGRATION ENCOURAGE EVOLUTION toward globally free trade, or does it place obstacles in its way, and perhaps even increase the likelihood of trade wars between competing blocs? The stakes in the bet as to whether RIAs are stepping stones to multilateral trade liberalization or millstones around its neck are truly huge.[1] Opening trade and increasing competition have been behind virtually every sustained economic growth experience, and the unprecedented postwar growth of world output and income has clearly been allied to the growth of world trade and trade liberalization. Progress here affects everyone, and is particularly important for the small and medium economies that depend heavily on international trade, and are the principal beneficiaries of an orderly and nondiscriminatory trading regime.

This chapter takes up these issues. First, we investigate the external tariffs of RIAs, and ask whether there are reasons to believe that a world of relatively few large RIAs will have lower or higher tariffs than a world composed of a large number of separate countries. We then turn to the dynamics of the world trading system. Does the presence of RIAs create incentives for excluded countries to join existing RIAs, to form new RIAs of their own, or to change their external trade policy in other ways? What are the prospects for "open regionalism" as proposed by some APEC countries? This leads us into the effects of RIAs on multilateral trade negotiations—the rounds of GATT/WTO talks. Have RIAs prompted countries to initiate and become involved in these negotiations, and do they facilitate or impede successful outcomes of the talks? Finally, we turn to the rules of the WTO itself, and ask whether the WTO should treat RIAs differently from its present lax stance.

5.1 How RIAs Set External Tariffs

ARE THERE ANY REASONS TO BELIEVE THAT A WORLD OF trading blocs is likely to be more prone to high tariffs between blocs than a world of separate nations? Some commentators have foreseen doomsday scenarios in which "Fortress Europe" and other major trade blocs engage in trade wars, damaging to themselves and above all to excluded developing regions. Is there any basis for such views?

A famous insight on the possible effects of trade blocs on tariffs comes from Paul Krugman (1991a and 1991b).[2] He noted that trade barriers would be lowest—and consequently world income greatest—in two opposite circumstances. One is when there is a single world trade bloc containing all countries, that is, global free trade. The other is when trade policy is set by many small independent countries, each so small as to have no market power and no reason to deviate from free trade. However, between these extremes each trading bloc has an incentive to use external tariffs to try and improve its terms of trade (reducing trade volumes to drive up the price of exports and reduce the price of imports). This reduces world real income, which reaches a minimum for some intermediate number of trade blocs.[3] Extending the insight in a simple (and not very robust) example, Krugman suggested that the worst number of similar sized RIAs for world welfare was three. Each sets a tariff to try and turn the terms of trade in its own favor, but this can only be at the expense of other blocs. The "prisoners' dilemma" in tariffs is worst with three prisoners!

This paper sparked a large literature, and many counter-examples. Perhaps the most pertinent criticism of the analysis surrounds the fact that tariff setting and trade negotiations involve repeated interactions between the same countries or blocs, so that the simple logic of the prisoner's dilemma need not apply. Countries or blocs may be able to cooperate, particularly if they perceive that the cost of breaking an agreement on tariffs is a future trade war, with all the costs this imposes. Analysis of this situation (for example, Bond and Syropoulos 1996a and 1996b) suggests that as bloc sizes get larger the returns to cheating on a trade agreement grow, but so too does the loss from the resulting trade war. In some cases at least, the former effect dominates, with the result that it is more difficult to maintain free trade in a world of large trading blocs, suggesting that regionalism increases the likelihood of protection. Considerable caution needs to be employed in interpreting these results;

they are not very robust, and no consensus has emerged about the magnitude nor even the net direction of general effects.

Turning from the analytical arguments, what is the evidence on the external trade policy of countries in RIAs? We start by noting that WTO rules governing RIAs expressly forbid increases in trade barriers (see section 6 of this chapter). However, in practice, the rules can be circumvented, potentially allowing RIA formation to be associated with tariff increases. For many developing countries there is a wide gulf between their actual (applied) tariffs and the maxima committed to in their formal bindings in the GATT. For example, when Mexico nearly doubled tariffs on 503 imported items from non-NAFTA sources in 1995, it did so without violating any bindings. WTO rules are ambiguous and poorly enforced, and a determined government can make trade policy more restrictive in ways more or less immune to WTO disciplines—say, through antidumping actions or health regulations. Also, in a world edging toward general trade liberalization, we need to ask not only whether RIAs raised tariffs, but whether they caused them to fall less than they otherwise might have.

We can do this by comparing the external trade policy of RIAs with that of countries not members of effective RIAs. Foroutan (1998) undertook such a study across developing countries. She divides countries according to whether or not they are in "effective" RIAs, defined as having a material effect on the share of intrabloc trade in total trade, and compares aspects of their external trade policies.[4] Her main findings are:

- *Average applied tariffs and nontariff barrier coverage.* The Latin American RIAs now have among the lowest average tariffs and nontariff barrier coverage among developing countries and have achieved the greatest liberalization since the mid-1980s. Except for Chile, the small non-RIA group has made much less progress. Until 1994 neither RIA nor non-RIA countries in Africa had displayed much tariff liberalization, and the mean average tariff is almost the same between the two groups. The most liberal countries in the sample are the members of North-South RIAs—Israel, Mexico, and Turkey.
- *Uruguay Round Concessions.* Here the only feasible comparison is between the Latin America RIA group and all non-RIA countries. The former group cut its bound tariff by more and bound more of its tariffs in the Round than did the latter, although levels started, and remain, relatively high.

This work is useful for refuting the simple hypothesis that RIAs lead directly to protectionism and are consistent with the idea that regionalism helps to lock in previous liberalization. However, the jury is still out on the issue; evidently many countries were seeking to liberalize trade by regional, multilateral, and possibly also unilateral routes, and we are far from knowing whether incentives for the multilateral and unilateral are sharpened or blunted by following the regional route.

5.2 The Dynamics of Regionalism

IN CHAPTER 1 WE SAW THE EXPLOSIVE GROWTH OF RIAS IN RECENT years. Is this, in part at least, because of an underlying dynamic by which forming a RIA increases the incentive for outside countries to become members, and so on, until the world is completely divided into RIAs? The process has been termed "domino regionalism" by Baldwin (1995), who analyzes how, after three decades of resistance, three Scandinavian countries decided to seek EU membership in the late 1980s. Although they were still uncomfortable with the EU politically, the economic pressures from the Single Market Program and from EU expansion were overwhelming. Arguably, the same process occurred when Canada sought access to the U.S.-Mexican talks that eventually created NAFTA, and motivated several Latin American and Caribbean countries to seek accession afterward. The same happened with Chile and Bolivia seeking association with MERCOSUR, with Mediterranean countries racing to get Euro-Med Agreements, and even perhaps with a number of late entrants seeking membership in the Cross-Border Initiative in Africa.[5]

In part, the drive toward regional agreement is driven by positive example; countries perceive benefits of membership and act to join or set up RIAs. But in part, the force comes from perceived adverse effects of nonmembership.

The Costs of Nonmembership

Why might the existence of some RIAs create or increase incentives for other countries to join? One obvious reason is simply that countries perceive benefits of membership, and become increasingly unwilling to forgo them. But another, more malign reason, is that countries suffer from being left out, and it is this that creates the rush to join. So how does the existence of RIAs affect nonmember countries?

The first and most direct way in which nonmembers are affected is through the change in trade flows caused by a RIA, causing both the exports and imports of nonmember countries to be smaller than they otherwise would have been. Such changes do not necessarily have an adverse effect, although there are several circumstances when they will. One is when they lead to a terms-of-trade deterioration for excluded economies. That is, the fall in demand for their exports (and reduction in supply of imports) may reduce their export price (and raise their import price). We saw in chapter 3 that member countries have gained from this, and that excluded country loss is simply the other side of the coin. Another set of circumstances under which excluded countries will be harmed by the relative decline in their trade is if their trade flows are already too small, that is, if they are running at a level at which marginal benefits exceed marginal costs. This will happen if the excluded economies have their own restrictive trade policies in place. It will also happen if firms are operating in imperfectly competitive markets and are making a positive price-cost margin on each unit of sales. Losing sales in a RIA market might be particularly damaging to such firms, causing them to lose profits, and perhaps causing them to be unable to cover their fixed costs.

Probably more importantly, countries fear that firms may relocate in search of the benefits of a larger market. This is consistent with what actually happened to FDI in Europe. Following announcement of the Single Market Program in the late 1980s, FDI fell in every single EFTA country. In order to restore their share of FDI, the governments of EFTA had little choice but to accept the Single Market Program. All except Switzerland did this, either by applying for EU membership or by joining the European Economic Area. Only once they had announced these moves did FDI recover (Baldwin, Forslid, and Haaland 1996).

Another source of loss from nonmembership of RIAs is the risk attached to being isolated if a trade war occurs. Of course, all countries—inside or outside RIAs—will usually lose from a trade war, but countries in RIAs have the insurance of knowing that they will still have free trade with partner countries. Whalley (1996) undertakes some numerical simulations of the costs of being outside a bloc during a trade war, showing that they can be very sizable. He argues that this creates a strong insurance motive for being inside a large RIA.

The argument is not all one-sided, however. Against these losses, there are a number of sources of gains that the rest of the world might expect from the formation of a RIA. We saw in chapter 3 that a RIA might improve the supply side of the integrating economies—perhaps by improving policy, increasing firms' efficiency, and thereby raising income levels. Such supply-side improvements will tend to reduce the prices of products exported by the RIA. This will be beneficial to countries who import these goods, although damaging to competing exporters.

Generally all these third country effects are likely to be small, particularly when the RIA is between relatively small economies, but there are exceptions. The important role NAFTA seems to have played in mitigating Mexico's 1994 peso crisis clearly benefited the rest of the world.

Bloc Formation

If we accept that the existence of RIAs creates demand for additional RIA membership, the demand can be met either by formation of new RIAs or by expansion in the membership in existing ones. Expansion requires the permission of existing members, and we discuss it in the next subsection (on open regionalism). Formation of new blocs has been an important alternative, as is evident from the figures on new RIA notifications. The process of bloc formation has been analyzed by Frankel (1997). He studies a hypothetical world of many countries and four continents, with zero trading costs between countries within the same continent and positive costs between continents.[6] Starting from a situation in which each continent has a nondiscriminatory trade policy, any one continent could then improve its welfare by forming an FTA and imposing preferential tariffs. This would harm overseas producers since they would have to lower their prices to mitigate their loss of competitiveness, and would then suffer from the terms-of-trade decline. From here a second continent benefits by creating a RIA, switching a loss of welfare into gain, and thence a third continent, converting larger losses into smaller ones. Even the fourth continent gains by creating a RIA, although by then all continents are worse off than under nondiscriminatory policies. World welfare falls at every stage, but no continent has the incentive to undo the regionalism unilaterally.

Open Regionalism?

Open regionalism originated from APEC whose leaders envisioned a community based on openness and free exchange of goods, services, and investment.

The term open regionalism has been used in different ways, and with two quite distinct meanings. One is *unconditional nondiscriminatory liberalization (or concerted unilateralism)*. The idea is that as member states liberalize trade within the bloc, so they simultaneously cut trade barriers on imports from external countries as well. This was the definition of the early APEC advocates, who saw the coalition as a means of encouraging countries to liberalize together and so provide for each other some of the terms of trade and political economy benefits of a full GATT/WTO round. Relative to forming a RIA, the policy brings the additional gains of liberalizing external trade and thereby removing the source of trade diversion. Relative to a liberalization by a single country, the fact that it would be *concerted*, with all members liberalizing together, brings additional benefits as access for imports is eased, so firms get improved access to partner markets; this reduces the likelihood of liberalization leading to a terms-of-trade loss. However, despite these attractions, the idea of concerted unilateralism does not now seem likely to make headway. Within APEC, the United States is implacably opposed to the idea. More generally, the WTO system is so firmly based on the notion of trade liberalization being a concession (to be granted in return for some concession by trading partners) that the idea is unlikely to catch on.

A second, and quite different concept is *open access* whereby the RIA announces that any country willing to abide by its rules may join. In terms of the economics, such an arrangement is still preferential, giving discriminatory benefits to members. Its main importance would be as a stepping stone to multilateralism: Could an open access RIA attract an increasing number of members, to the point where almost all countries became members?

Analytical treatments of this issue are not optimistic. As we saw in chapter 4, there is generally an optimal size for a RIA, from the point of view of existing members, so it is not clear why members should want unrestricted access. In practical terms, the feasibility of open access depends crucially on the depth of the scheme. Where a RIA involves few conditions, then open access can be quite easily envisaged. Perhaps the best example is the Cross-Border Initiative in East and southern Africa, in which neither internal preferences nor external tariff harmonization are rigorously enforced. But for deeper agreements, open access is harder to envisage.

NAFTA, where the principal rules are completely free trade in goods and open investment, might seem to be a candidate, but has in fact rejected many overtures. This seems more to avoid adjustment in the United States than because other issues such as quotas for professional migration or dispute settlement require negotiation. MERCOSUR has expressed willingness to accept new members, implying a degree of open access. However, given that fairly deep integration is planned, detailed negotiation is required. Association—the status preferred by Chile— is easier, but does not offer full integration and still requires several years of talks.

The EU stands ready to sign association agreements with many neighboring countries, and ostensibly with the African, Caribbean, and Pacific countries, but only on its own terms covering issues such as rules of origin, excluded sectors, the use of antidumping duties, and so on. Full membership in the EU is anything but open access. The United Kingdom had to ask three times before it was allowed to join, and Turkey was rejected until recently. Negotiations are tortuous once accession is agreed in principle. Each of the five current Eastern European candidates faces a formidable list of demands and requirements prior to membership. In several cases they are required to adopt policies from which some existing members have negotiated exemptions (such as the Social Chapter). Still, EU membership has increased from 6 to 15 countries and is expected to increase to 25 countries over the next decade or so.

In practice, what we are seeing here is essentially that any country is free to apply; but the price of entry is set separately for each entrant. This can lead to asymmetric agreements in which benefits to developing country candidates are reduced and possibly appropriated by existing members through side conditions on issues such as the environment, labor regulations, and rules of origin. Since the more complex aspects of RIAs—especially those with budgetary implications—*have* to be negotiated, access can never be automatic and unconditional. In practice, it will not be easy for the WTO to write or enforce general rules for open access, and it is unlikely that this route will lead to ever expanding membership.

However, even though full and unconditional open access to RIAs is unlikely to be feasible, increased access by developing countries to the markets of the trade blocs in the industrial North is more likely through a successful WTO or through association agreements with the EU, the United States, or Japan. The latter requires the WTO to modify its rules regarding RIAs and create a presumptive right of association. As with the most favored nation (MFN) clause, if association is granted to one country, there should be a presumption that it should be available to others. For instance, if Iceland is offered reciprocal freedom from anti-dumping suits by the EU, the same option should be available to Ghana. In practice, association is complex and each accession needs to be negotiated, but the poor should not be automatically denied association rights provided to middle-income countries by the EU and NAFTA. This issue is examined in more detail in section 5.6.

What about APEC itself, where the idea originated? It has yet really to decide between these alternatives, because there has not yet been any APEC liberalization. Members have certainly not yet introduced any discriminatory trade policies (with the minor exception of the APEC business visa), but neither have they yet moved beyond implementing their Uruguay obligations and, for developing members, their own unilateral reforms. The manifesto still contains a commitment to global liberalization, but it is worth recalling that, although more positive in its approach and timetable, this manifesto is not very different from the EEC's 1957 statement that "by establishing a customs union between themselves, member states aim to contribute, in the common interest, to the harmonious development of world trade, the progressive abolition of restrictions on international trade and the lowering of customs barriers" (Article 110.1, Treaty of Rome).

5.3 Regionalism and Multilateral Trade Negotiations

ONE OF THE MAIN VEHICLES FOR TRADE LIBERALIZATION HAS been the series of GATT/WTO rounds of trade negotiations. From the late 1940s through the present, these rounds have reduced average tariff rates on manufactures from more than 40 percent to less than 5 percent. How do RIAs impact on multilateral trade negotiations? Do they promote the initiation and conclusion of these rounds, or provide obstacles to their progress? Three sorts of arguments have been made.

Multilateralism as a Response to Regionalism

The first argument is that countries outside RIAs may react to their exclusion by attempting to accelerate multilateral liberalization. Many commentators suggest that the creation of the EEC in 1957 had this effect. This, they suggest, led directly to the Dillon and Kennedy Rounds of GATT negotiations as the United States sought to mitigate the EEC's potential for diverting trade (Lawrence 1991; Sapir 1993; WTO 1995). Although perfectly conceivable, this is not a straightforward argument.

First, it seems unlikely that multilateral negotiations would have stopped completely had the EEC not been created, especially given the global reach of the United States during the 1960s. Thus, at most, the EEC affected the timing, not the occurrence, of the Rounds. Second, agriculture played an important role in the formation of the EEC, and the EEC was probably more successful in resisting that sector's liberalization in the multilateral trade negotiations than its individual members would have been. This has probably made future liberalization more, not less, difficult. Third, suppose that the hypothesis were true, that the creation of the EEC had led to negotiations. The logic of the argument is essentially coercive: EEC members did something that their trading partners considered harmful, and then offered to mitigate it in return for concessions. Coercion may be warranted and the outcome may have been beneficial, but this is a dangerous game. It depends critically on the willingness of the partners to fold—(by negotiating) rather than fight (by raising tariffs) and to respond multilaterally rather than regionally.

It has also been argued that regionalism was behind the Tokyo Round. Winham (1986) reports both the first EEC enlargement (including free trade with EFTA) and the restrictiveness of Europe's Common Agricultural Policy as factors in the United States desire for a Round . The former observation seems no more compelling than those surrounding the creation of the EEC, while the latter is distinctly two-edged: it is based on regionalism having increased trade restrictions in agriculture (Common Agricultural Policy), and a response to this being negotiation. For the net effect of this on multilateral progress to be beneficial requires a negotiating structure in which might and countervailing power are the critical elements of liberalization.

Finally, consider the Uruguay Round, of which the WTO (1995) says, "There is little doubt that...the spread of regionalism [was a] major factor in eliciting the concessions needed to conclude" the Round. There was, indeed, a perception that the failure of the Round would lead to regional fragmentation. This almost certainly encouraged the spread of defensive regionalism, but whether this pressured the two major parties to agree is not clear, for they were the prime "regionalists," and they would certainly not have been the principal casualties of fragmentation. Some senior EU negotiators have said that the 1993 Seattle APEC Summit induced the EU finally to concede on agriculture and conclude the Uruguay Round (Bergsten 1997). Again, this may be true, but there are counter-arguments. For example, APEC was not advertised as a discriminatory RIA, and any discrimination would, anyway, have been far in the future. Also, the principal necessary condition for the EU to complete the round was agricultural reform, which was initiated in 1990 and completed in 1992 (Hathaway and Ingco 1996).

Does Regionalism Facilitate Negotiation?

If regional integration agreements made trade negotiations easier, perhaps they would help the world evolve toward freer trade. Coordinated coalitions may have greater negotiating power than their members do individually and such coalitions may facilitate progress just by reducing the number of players represented in a negotiation (Kahler 1995). Whether this really occurs is a moot point. For example, a negotiation comprising one dominant partner and a competitive fringe of small countries might be easier and proceed further than if the fringe coalesced into a significant counterforce.

This line of reasoning prejudges the issue of whether blocs are genuinely unified in their approach to trade negotiations. This is not usually so, meaning that any gains from having fewer players in the last stage of a negotiation are offset by the complexity of agreeing joint positions in the first phase. The difficulties of achieving a European position on agriculture and cultural protection in the Uruguay Round are well known, and formulating EEC positions in the Tokyo Round proved complex (Winham 1986). Moreover, two-stage negotiations need not be more liberal than single-stage ones (Basevi, Delbono, and Mariotti 1995). To be sure, Germany and the United Kingdom pressured France to agree to the agricultural deal in the Uruguay Round, but the liberalizers had to make potentially trade-restricting concessions on "commercial defense instruments" to clinch the deal. Wang and Winters (1998) argue that the benefits to African countries of enhancing their bargaining power by cooperation are likely to be outweighed by the costs of combining their different interests into a single negotiating position.

While the EU has internal procedures for arriving at a common position, many of the CUs that attend the next round of global trade talks have not yet developed procedures for determining their negotiating positions. SACU's previous practice of delegating all responsibility to South Africa begins to look less tenable as divisions emerge between members, and MERCOSUR has yet to devise really robust internal decisionmaking capacity. Thus, at least into the foreseeable future, RIAs do not seem likely to facilitate even a traditional trade negotiation. Moreover, as WTO has extended its reach, it has embraced subjects in which most central CU authorities have no mandate to negotiate. Mixing national and CU responsibilities seems unlikely to simplify matters, and it is not realistic to expect member countries to surrender sovereignty on sensitive issues to regional bodies just because trade negotiations are in process.

Successful trade negotiations also require political will and administrative effort. Reserves of administrative skill, political capital, or imagination are finite; if they are devoted to a RIA they are not available for multilateral objectives. These arguments were advanced to explain both EU and U.S. behavior during the Uruguay Round, but they must be several times more important for developing countries. Negotiating a RIA, especially with a major power that has its own objectives, will absorb a huge proportion of the scarce policymaking skills of a developing country. Perhaps one of the opportunity-costs of RIAs is that less negotiating capacity and political capital are available for multilateral negotiations.

One alarming possibility is that regionalism might undermine U.S. or EU willingness to participate actively in the multilateral system.[7] Over the last three decades they have been major players, monitoring both smaller countries' policies and each other's. A loss of interest by either would reduce WTO's overall effectiveness and could upset the current fine balance.

Regionalism and the Frontiers of Liberalization

One of the strengths that is frequently claimed for the regional approach to liberalization is that it makes it easier to handle the tough issues (Kahler 1995); there are areas in which regional liberalization or harmonization between similar or like-minded countries is feasible when multilateral progress is not. As we have seen (chapter 4) the EU has addressed a wide range of "deep integration" issues; NAFTA has tackled investment; Brazil has free trade in information technology goods within MERCOSUR; Chile and Canada have eschewed antidumping actions on mutual trade.[8]

But until recently even RIAs among industrial countries, let alone those among developing ones, had not advanced much further with liberalization than had the multilateral system (Hoekman and Leidy 1993). Thus, for example, agriculture frequently remained restricted, transport, culture, and other sensitive services were excluded; and government procurement was ignored de facto if not de jure. The EU, especially in the Single Market Program, has now advanced further, but this took 30 years to initiate and is, to date, unique. Overall, RIAs have not led on the tough issues to the extent that is sometimes supposed.

The benefit of having RIAs tackle these "tough issues" depends heavily on whether they are liberalizing and whether they are otherwise well-suited to developing country needs and capacities. The EU has used the Europe Agreements to obtain action on environmental and labor conditions and on intellectual property, and the United States has used NAFTA as a tool for enforcing Mexican labor and environmental standards. It is quite possible that practices developed by the major RIAs will not suit developing countries well, and may also be less open and liberal.

An extension of the "tough issues" argument is that RIAs help develop blueprints for subsequent multilateral negotiations (Bergsten 1996). For example, the EU pioneered "bulk" mutual recognition for industrial standards and services harmonization, and NAFTA's investment chapter may inform a multilateral investment negotiation (if there is one). On the other hand, the EEC also suggested the Common Agricultural Policy as a model for agriculture in the Kennedy Round. Once again then, the blueprints might not suit developing countries well. There is the further danger that coming to negotiations with a fully developed blueprint can appear to be a pressure tactic that actually makes negotiation more difficult; developing countries' de facto rejections of the OECD draft Multilateral Agreement on Investment in 1998 contains at least an element of this.

Overall then, we find the arguments that regionalism has promoted or facilitated multilateral trade negotiations to be rather weak. There is little evidence that RIAs have either prompted or facilitated negotiations, and real dangers that they might dilute countries' involvement in such negotiations.

5.4 Regionalism and the WTO

THE PREVIOUS ANALYSIS SUGGESTS THAT INTERNATIONAL policy toward regionalism should aim to:

- Encourage RIAs to achieve trade creation and avoid trade diversion, both for the sake of members and to minimize harm to excluded countries, for instance, by setting low external tariffs
- Permit deep integration, including nation building, between members
- Preserve the effects of previous liberalization and provide credibility for any liberalization that form part of the RIA
- Support a liberalizing dynamic within member countries and in the world trading system as a whole.

The instrument we have for international policy on regionalism is the WTO, and this section explores how it manages regionalism and whether its rules could be reformed to help it do better.[9] RIAs are officially sanctioned—but conditional—exceptions to the GATT's rules on nondiscrimination. The conditions imposed on RIA formation doubtless constrain and mold the pattern of regionalism in the world, but they are neither adequate, nor adequately enforced, to ensure that regionalism is economically beneficial for either its members or excluded countries. The responsibility for good outcomes falls on governments themselves; they cannot tie their own or each other's hands sufficiently tightly in the WTO to preclude the possibilities of signing harmful RIAs.

The world trade system works—pragmatically and consensually. The GATT was created in 1947 as a temporary body to assist countries in trade liberalization. Its role was to codify and record a series of tariff reductions that its members wished to make, and provide a structure to give credibility to those reductions. It discouraged the reversal or nullification of tariff cuts by restricting policies that impose duties on an ad hoc basis, such as antidumping duties and emergency protection, and equivalent policies such as internal taxes on imports. It also defined important mechanics of trade, such as the valuation of trade for customs purposes. A key concept of the GATT, indeed the cornerstone of the present world trading system, is nondiscrimination between different sources of the same imported good, which is achieved by requiring members to give each other MFN treatment, except in specified circumstances. With an assurance of nondiscrimination, when A negotiates a reduction in one of B's tariffs, it knows that the commercial value of its effort will not be undermined by B then offering C an even lower tariff. This, in turn, makes A more willing to "buy" the concession by reducing one of its own tariffs on B, and so encourages trade liberalization.

Over 50 years of operation the GATT continued in this low-key, member-driven, fashion. It was essentially consensual in approach and pragmatic in operation. The GATT did not adjudicate trade disputes, but had a dispute settlement process, less concerned with law than with solving disputes in a way that preserved consensus and allowed the liberalizing bandwagon to continue to roll. The WTO, which was created in 1995 to oversee the GATT and certain other agreements, is more legalistic, but still focuses heavily on pragmatic and mutually acceptable solutions to problems. The WTO/GATT administers a set of rules for behavior, not a set of outcomes—it is concerned with meeting agreed obligations and rights rather than with economic outcomes per se. The WTO/GATT has undoubtedly been a force for economic good, but its role has not been defined in those terms.

The GATT traditionally did not intrude into domestic politics. It had no ability to force member countries to liberalize if they did not wish to, and was extremely light-handed in its requirements about the shape of domestic legislation. The WTO is rather more far-reaching; through its greater breadth and its "single undertaking," under which members must subscribe to virtually all its rules, rather than, as previously, treat some as optional extras, it has constrained governments more tightly. Nevertheless, the WTO can still be effective only if it proceeds more or less by consensus.

Given this background, the WTO can enhance the economic well-being of developing countries in four ways. First, if sufficient members wish, it can organize periodic rounds of tariff negotiations that offer opportunities and incentives to members to reduce their barriers to trade. Second, it provides guidelines for domestic policy—directly in some cases, but more often indirectly by shaping the terms of the debate. Governments resisting pressures to protect particular lobbying groups are immeasurably strengthened if they can point to prohibitions in the WTO agreements. Third, the WTO can protect the rights of members against certain rules violations by other members. It cannot necessarily, however, protect members against harm.[10] Fourth, it provides a forum and mechanism for governments to manage the spillovers from members' trade policies onto their partners. These four links provide the framework for assessing the WTO's current rules about RIAs and exploring whether they can be improved.

5.5 The Rules for RIAs

ARTICLE XXIV OF THE GATT SETS LIMITS ON THE RIGHTS OF RIA member countries to violate the MFN principle. It imposes three principal restrictions (appendix 1). A RIA must:

- Not "on the whole" raise protection against excluded countries
- Reduce internal tariffs to zero and remove "other restrictive regulations of commerce" other than those justified by other GATT articles
- Cover "substantially all trade."

These conditions ensure that RIAs do not undermine the access of other countries to the RIA market. The first preserves the sanctity of tariff bindings by ensuring that forming a RIA does not result in a wholesale dissolution of previous bindings. It is supplemented by a rule that compensation is due to individual partners for tariff increases induced by the RIA if other reductions to keep the average constant do not maintain a fair balance of concessions. Together with the 1994 Uruguay Round Understanding on the Interpretation of Article XXIV on how to measure tariff barriers for RIAs, these provisions offer reasonable assurances that the barriers facing nonmembers will not be raised.

The second condition helps defend the MFN principle by making it subject to an "all-or-nothing" exception. If countries were free to negotiate different levels of preference with each trading partner, binding and nondiscrimination would be fatally undermined: no member could be sure that it would receive the benefits it expected from negotiating and reciprocating for a partner's tariff reduction. Also, if a customs union is a first step toward nation building, it is inappropriate for an international trade treaty to stand in the way of such progress. Thus, internal free trade, such as one (usually) achieves within a single country, would seem to be an acceptable derogation of MFN, whereas preferences would not. The third condition reinforces this by requiring a serious degree of commitment to a RIA in terms of sectors.

The second and third conditions—no internal tariffs and substantial coverage—are important in heading off pressure to use tariffs to fine-tune political favoritism toward either domestic industries or partner countries; they help to prevent governments that restrict RIAs from swapping trade-diverting concessions and, thus, from avoiding politically more painful trade creation. These conditions essentially require a serious commitment to integrating member markets as a condition for proceeding.

Article XXIV is generally an aid to better RIAs, but it is certainly not sufficient for good economic policy. Even if the conditions were applied without exception they would not preclude harmful RIAs: Wholly GATT-compatible RIAs can be predominantly trade diverting, excluded countries can suffer terms-of-trade declines, and institutions can arise that make liberal policies less likely.

There are major difficulties in interpreting the conditions of Article XXIV. Even following the Uruguay Round Understanding there is no agreement about what "substantially all trade" means, nor even whether it refers to the proportion of actual trade covered or the inclusion of all major sectors of the economy. Similarly the treatment of nontariff barriers in assessing the overall level of trade restriction is not defined, nor is that of rules of origin. The requirement that "other restrictive regulations of commerce" be removed between members is ambiguously worded: several exceptions to this requirement are identified explicitly but other barriers, including antidumping duties and emergency protection, are not. Complete integration between members of a RIA would abolish these barriers and so their continuation—in NAFTA or the Euro-Med agreements—suggests an unwillingness to proceed too far in that direction.

Perhaps because of its ambiguities, Article XXIV has been notoriously weakly enforced. RIAs have to be notified to the GATT and until 1996, each was then reviewed by an ad hoc working party to see if it was in conformity with the Article. WTO (1995) reports that of 69 working parties reporting up to and including 1994, only 6 were able to agree that a RIA met the requirements of Article XXIV, of which only CARICOM and Czech-Slovak CU remain operative. However, the remainder did not conclude that agreements were not in conformity—they merely left the matter undetermined.

This agnosticism is essentially the product of the GATT's consensual nature. The first major test of the article was the Treaty of Rome establishing the EEC. The political pressure to permit it was enormous: EEC countries would almost certainly have put the EEC before the GATT in the event of conflict and the United States strongly supported the treaty. The treaty, however, clearly violated Article XXIV, and so the only feasible solution was not to push the review to conclusion.[11] Given a start like this, the EEC's willingness to support more or less any RIA in the GATT, the need for working parties to reach consensus, and the GATT's inability to make an adverse determination without the acquiescence of the party at fault,[12] it is hardly surprising that future reviews proved little more demanding. Nor have matters improved with the establishment in 1996 of a single Committee on Regional Trading Agreements to conduct the reviews. The inability to rule on whether RIAs conform to article XXIV does not mean that the rules have had no effect, for we do not know the extent to which they have influenced the structure of RIAs that have come forward, nor which potential arrangements they have discouraged.[13] It is not an encouraging record, however, either from the point of view of enforcing current rules or from that of rewriting the rules to increase their ability to distinguish good from bad RIAs.

Finally, Articles XXIV.10 and XXV of the GATT can be used to grant waivers to make otherwise inadmissible policies GATT-legal. This was done for the European Coal and Steel Community (1952) and the U.S.-Canada Auto Pact (1965). Under WTO, waivers are still feasible but are time-limited.

Article XXIV of the GATT refers to trade in goods. The equivalent for services is Article V of the GATS, which is modeled closely on it. The requirement not to raise barriers to third countries is rather tighter: it is applied sector by sector rather than "on the whole," and third country suppliers already engaged in "substantive business" in a RIA territory before the RIA is concluded must receive RIA treatment. The "substantially all trade" ambiguity is only slightly abated, with an explicit note that the word "substantially" be "understood in terms of number of sectors, volume of trade, and modes of supply." For covered sectors "substantially all discrimination" is to be removed, but since this is defined as comprising elimination of barriers *or* prohibition on new or more discriminatory barriers, or both, it need amount to very little.[14] Developing countries receive "flexibility" on "substantially all" discrimination and exemption from the need to give RIA treatment to least third country firms with "substantial business" in member countries.

The Rules for Developing Countries

If all this were not enough, a further complication for developing countries is an "Enabling Clause"[15] introduced in 1979 that significantly relaxes the conditions for creating RIAs that include only developing countries. It drops the conditions on the coverage of trade, and allows developing countries to reduce tariffs on mutual trade in any way they wish, and nontariff measures "in accordance with criteria which may be prescribed" by the WTO members. It then supplements the first condition with the nonoperational requirement that the RIA not constitute a barrier to MFN tariff reductions or cause "undue difficulties" for other contracting parties.

In practice, developing countries have had virtual carte blanche. Twelve preferential arrangements have been notified under the Enabling Clause, including the Latin American Integration Association, ASEAN, and the GCC. Internal preferences of 25 percent and 50 percent figured in ASEAN's trading plans and also in many of the arrangements concluded under the Latin American Integration Association and in the GCC. There is little sign that internal preferences have undermined MFN agreements with other trading partners but then, until recently, these countries did not make many MFN agreements. Indeed, until the late 1980s, the Latin American and African countries' frequent use of regional arrangements and weak participation in the multilateral rounds might suggest a substitution of one form of liberalization for the other. More worrying were the sectoral agreements that abounded in Latin America.

The Enabling Clause dilutes the weak discipline that Article XXIV imposes. Even if Article XXIV does not actually stop many harmful practices, it does at least avoid automatically giving them the respectability of legal cover. Thus, while the GATT knowingly and willingly permitted Latin American Free Trade Area (1960) and the initial notification of ASEAN (1977) to violate Article XXIV (Finger 1993), at least it required continuing consultation with partners and left open the possibility of challenge in the dispute settlement process. The Enabling Clause offers more cover in various areas, and thus erodes even this discipline.[16]

Reform of the Rules?

The WTO rules on RIAs are not exactly broken, but they are creaky, and it is worth asking what might be done about them. We focus here on their economic content, and on the feasibility of reform. Feasibility seems to be a more binding constraint than devising economically sensible rules. Indeed, major political backing for tightening looks improbable, as few countries within RIAs appear to seek tighter discipline, as the EU continues its Mediterranean agreements and considers replacing the trade provisions of the Lomé Convention with an FTA, and as the United States contemplates the Free Trade Area of the Americas.[17] However, see section 5.6 for a proposal on changing rules for both industrial and developing countries.

A RIA that does not reduce external barriers may cause trade diversion. One discipline on this would be to require RIA members to liberalize, both to reduce diversion and to induce external trade creation with nonmembers. Finger (1993) views these reductions as a price to be negotiated to persuade nonmembers to forgo their MFN rights. How far the parties are prepared to go in a negotiation, however, is determined by the prevailing rules and enforcement mechanisms that define the outcome if negotiations fail; unfortunately, these currently leave nonmembers almost no negotiating power. Hence other authors have made more concrete proposals.

Bhagwati (1993) suggests requiring that for each tariff heading a CU's common external tariff be bound at the minimum tariff for that heading among all members. This does not guarantee the elimination of trade diversion—suppose the tariffs of three members were 98 percent, 99 percent, and 100 percent—but it will clearly reduce it. It would impose a high (mercantilist) price on RIA formation, so only "serious" integrators would pay it, and would, overall, be quite trade-liberalizing. As a reform it is admirably clear, and if feasible, it would be desirable economically. Its demanding nature, however, makes it very unlikely to succeed in the present circumstances.

Related is a proposal that members of FTAs be required to bind their tariffs at actual applied rates on the eve of the RIA. Apart from what this might do to pre-FTA applied rates, this suggestion is random in its liberalizing effect, which reduces its moral force. Bhagwati would just ban FTAs. This is also consistent with seeking to restrict RIAs to those that are committed to far-reaching integration, but again faces severe feasibility constraints, especially since some FTAs proceed quite far in other directions.

Tied up with the FTA question is that of rules of origin. Some suggest a requirement that they be no more restrictive than before the RIA, but this is difficult to determine, ad hoc, manipulable in nature, and potentially very complex in the face of technological changes. Better would be a requirement precluding the manipulation of such rules for protectionist purposes, such as that countries should adhere to a single set of rules of origin agreed internationally, or that a country's preferential rules should be the same as its nonpreferential ones. Wonnacott (1996) suggests a number of milder reforms in this direction: for example, that rules of origin be banned where tariffs differ between members by less than, say, 2 percentage points, or that for each commodity they be banned for the FTA member with the lowest tariff. These might be acceptable, but would only scratch the surface.

One proposal has been made to adopt *ex post* reviews to determine whether nonmember exports have fallen since a RIA was created and demand changes in policies if they have (McMillan 1993). Although frequently taken seriously (for example, Frankel 1997), the proposal is wrong in virtually every respect. Exports are the wrong criterion, quantitative targets are the wrong way to formulate trade policy, the internal costs of trade diversion are ignored, economic modeling is still too imprecise to identify causes with any credibility, and *ex post* adjustment after five years is no basis for the policy predictability sought by investors.

There are three major proposals for creating a "liberal dynamic." Srinivasan (1998) proposes that RIAs be permitted only temporarily by requiring all RIA concessions to be extended to all countries within, say, five years. This is effectively a ban on RIAs, and certainly foregoes any gains that they might offer in terms of deep integration or nation building. It is not a serious contender.

Second, stretching back at least to the United States submission to the Preparatory Committee of London Monetary and Economic Conference of 1933, scholars and policymakers have argued that requiring RIAs to admit any country willing to accept their rules both reduces their adverse effects on excluded countries and establishes a liberal dynamic (Viner 1950). While this may be true if admission can be guaranteed, virtually every RIA extant has geographical restrictions on membership and has features that require negotiation. The latter vitiate the promise of "open access." However, though unconditional open access seems unfeasible, section 5.6 suggests a way to improve developing countries' access to the large blocs in the North.

A more feasible approach than unconditional open access is to define and enforce current rules more rigorously. A precise definition and enforcement of "substantially all trade" would be a useful innovation. A quantitative indicator would be clear, but it would need to be high given that the kinds of trade restrictions countries wish to maintain typically constrain existing trade quite fiercely. The frequently cited 80 percent, which dates from consideration of the Treaty of Rome is not adequate. Even 90 percent, which seems to inform current EU-MERCOSUR talks, is not indicative of serious intent to integrate. We would advocate 95 percent after 10 years and 98 percent after 15 years. Similarly, a more constraining view of "other restrictive regulations of commerce" would be useful—ensuring that they include the effects of rules of origin on excluded countries, and that obvious barriers such as safeguards actions and antidumping duties are abolished internally. The latter requirement would increase the degree of trade creation, since these policies are explicitly aimed at preserving domestic output levels. Thus they would raise the bar for "serious" regionalism.

However, even these changes might encounter fierce opposition and will require major political commitment by many WTO members to be implemented. To be acceptable to the major powers, they will certainly need to be accompanied by a grandfathering clause to assure current RIAs that they will not be undermined by new interpretations.

A vehicle to take forward reform measures is the Committee on Regional Trading Agreements (CRTA), which reports to the WTO's General Council, and was established in 1996 to increase the transparency, efficiency, and consistency of the WTO's treatment of RIAs. It was seen as a means of ensuring more rigorous review of new RIAs because a single group would review all of them using the same criteria and with more searching notification and information requirements. It would also undertake periodic review of existing RIAs, and could resolve some of the systemic issues that remained after the Uruguay Round. The more thorough review was seen as a route to better compliance with WTO requirements, while the consideration of conceptual issues was a step toward refining and codifying the rules more precisely.

Unfortunately the CRTA has not yet reached its stride. Its assessments of particular cases have been stymied by the lack of clear systemic rules, and the discussion of rules stalemated on exactly the same "substantially all" and "other regulations" issues as the previous Uruguay Round discussions. By December 1997 the Committee had initiated consideration of 59 RIAs (including 32 inherited from previous working parties). It had completed factual analysis of 30 of these, and was "elaborating conclusions" on 26. To date, no analyses have been released or conclusions reached.

The future development of the CRTA could take several routes. Review of existing RIAs is not likely to be productive. Although RIAs are open to dispute if third party countries feel aggrieved (at least until the

CRTA has formally certified their WTO-conformity), the rules seeking serious intent to integrate are not really susceptible to this process. Non-member countries are unlikely to press RIAs to include more sectors when they expect this to increase trade diversion. Similarly, why would a nonmember country seek to free RIA members from the threat of each other's antidumping legislation? Members do not normally bring internal disputes to the WTO.[18]

When it comes to new RIAs, one possibility is to have a detailed case-by-case study of the likely effects to the RIA. But the CRTA faces a serious timing problem. Unless agreements are submitted to the WTO early in the process of negotiation—in which case they will be very provisional—reviews will generally be too late to influence their initial form. Otherwise, reviews will be too late to affect public debate and will, if they call for changes, upset carefully negotiated compromises. For that reason they will be resisted and resented by members, which is bad news for a consensual organization. Thus considerable political courage will be called for to enforce CRTA findings until their requirements are sufficiently understood and respected by members to be met *ab initio*. This process of review and response would have to be aided by detailed economic studies of RIAs stretching well beyond the legalities of Articles XXIV and V.

The better way forward is for review of new RIAs to be restricted to ensuring compliance with the tighter Article XXIV rules on liberalization of "substantially all trade" and "other restrictive regulations of commerce" which we proposed above. As we have argued, these rules would raise the bar for "serious regionalism," while leaving it clear that WTO approval does not validate the economic benefits of a RIA for its members. The responsibility for good RIAs lies with governments themselves.

5.6 Post-Seattle

THE FAILURE OF WTO MEMBERS TO AGREE TO A NEW ROUND of negotiations at the Ministerial in Seattle in December 1999 has dealt a blow to the WTO. One of the dangers is likely to be that developing country members that were thinking of fuller participation in the WTO and were considering further unilateral trade liberalization and binding their lower tariffs at the WTO may have become further disappointed by the multilateral system after Seattle and may be looking more seriously at regional options. As examined in the report, RIAs among developing countries are unlikely to provide the benefits available in North-South RIAs or in the multilateral system. Developing countries have much to gain from multilateral liberalization as enforced by the MFN clause: it strengthens weaker countries by limiting the ability of stronger ones to make deals with each other that exclude the weaker ones.

In order to more fully integrate the developing countries in the multilateral system and make it work for them, simply extending the disciplines of Articles XXIV and V to their RIAs will not work. We believe a quid pro quo is necessary where industrial countries offer something in return for the developing countries' acceptance of these disciplines.

Mike Moore, secretary-general of the WTO, argued at the January 2000 United Nations Conference on Trade and Development-X Conference in Bangkok that richer nations need to bring down trade barriers to exports from developing countries. In his presentation he stated that, "It makes no sense to spend extra billions on enhanced debt relief if, at the same time, the ability of poorer countries to achieve debt sustainability is impeded by a lack of access for their exports." James Wolfensohn, president of the World Bank, provided a similar message.

Industrial countries are trying to help developing countries through foreign aid, technical assistance, and debt forgiveness, especially to the heavily indebted poor countries. What is the logic in providing foreign aid, debt forgiveness, and other assistance, but not opening up markets in order to help developing countries expand their exports and get out from under these large debt burdens? Moreover, the least-developed countries export mostly products that do not compete with OECD industries, and the GNP of all these countries put together does not even amount to that of a mid-sized European country. Thus, the cost of opening markets to these countries would be small for the OECD and would help ensure that these countries continue with their own unilateral liberalization efforts by enabling them to obtain more benefits from liberalization.

The poor need secure access to the North and they can get this in only two ways: through a successful WTO pursuing multilateral nonpreferential liberalization as enforced by the MFN clause, or through association agreements with the EU, NAFTA, or Japan. These are, in fact, the two different uses of the term "open regionalism": concerted multilateralism, and open access to membership of the Northern clubs. The poor can both support the WTO against the menace of Northern protectionist lobbies and at the same time pressure for the right of access to the clubs.

We have proposed that the WTO should modify its rules concerning trade blocs to create a presumptive right of association. Analogous to the MFN clause, if association is granted to one country, there should be a presumption that similar terms should be available to others: if Iceland is offered reciprocal freedom from antidumping suits by the EU, then the same option should be available to Ghana. Naturally, association is complex, and so in practice each accession must be negotiated; regardless, the poor should not be denied the association rights already conferred on several middle-income countries.

We have proposed a package negotiating offer by the South to the North concerning the WTO rules governing trade blocs. The South would offer to extend the existing rules concerning North-North trade blocs to South-South blocs. Although this is a concession, it would strengthen the MFN principle that is very much in the interest of the South. In return, the South would demand an open access rule, in which the right to equal treatment of applications for association in all trade blocs would be enshrined.

5.7 Conclusion

THE CONCLUSION FIRST DEALS WITH CHANGES IN WTO RULES to benefit developing countries, and second, with improvement and enforcement of rules. We first recommend that:

- Industrial countries should fully open their markets to developing country exports, particularly those from least-developing countries.
- The WTO should modify its rules concerning trade blocs to create a presumptive right of association.
- In return, developing countries should accept the disciplines of Articles XXIV and V for their RIAs.

Second, we recommend that:

- The WTO enforce the disciplines of Articles XXIV and V rigorously in the CRTA, especially those on coverage and depth of liberalization.
- The WTO define the rules more rigorously: On "substantially all trade," we advocate 95 percent of trade after 10 years and 98 percent after 15; on "other restrictive regulations of commerce," we

advocate inclusion of the abolition of internal barriers, such as safe-guard actions and antidumping duties.

- The WTO use the dispute settlement procedure to enforce the rights of third countries not to face increases in protection either directly or indirectly through the use of tools such as rules of origin.

Appendix I: WTO Provisions on Regional Integration Arrangements (Extracts)

Article XXIV of GATT

4. The contracting parties…also recognize that the purpose of a cus-toms union or of a free trade area should be to facilitate trade be-tween the constituent territories and not to raise barriers to trade.

5(a). With respect to a customs union…the duties and other regula-tions of commerce imposed at the institution…shall not on the whole be higher or more restrictive than the general incidence of the duties and regulations of commerce applicable in the constitu-ent territories prior to the formation of such union…

(b). With respect to a free trade area…the duties and other regulations of commerce maintained in each of the constituent territories and applicable at the formation of such free-trade area…shall not be higher or more restrictive than the corresponding duties and other regulations of commerce existing in the same constituent territo-ries prior to the formation of the free-trade area…

(c). Any interim agreement…shall include a plan and schedule for the formation of such a customs union or of such a free-trade area within a reasonable length of time.

7(a). Any contracting party deciding to enter into a customs union or a free-trade area, shall promptly notify the CONTRACTING PARTIES and shall make available to them such information…

8(a). A customs union shall be understood to mean the substitution of a single customs territory for two or more customs territories, so that: (i) duties and other restrictive regulations of commerce (ex-cept, where necessary, those permitted under Article XI, XII, XIII, XIV, XV and XX) are eliminated with respect to…substantially all the trade in products originating in such territories…

8(b). A free trade area shall be understood to mean a group of two or more customs territories in which the duties and other restrictive regulations of commerce (except, where necessary, those permitted under Articles XI, XII, XIII, XIV, XV and XX) are eliminated on substantially all the trade between the constituent territories in products originating in such territories.

The Enabling Clause

1. Notwithstanding the provisions of Article I...contracting parties may accord differential and more favorable treatment to developing countries, without according such treatment to other contracting parties.

2(c). The provisions of paragraph 1 apply to the...regional or global arrangements entered into amongst less-developed contracting parties for the mutual reduction or elimination of tariffs and, in accordance with criteria or conditions which may be prescribed by the CONTRACTING PARTIES, for the mutual reduction or elimination of nontariff measures, on products imported from one other;

The Uruguay Round Understanding on the Interpretation of Article XXIV

2. The evaluation...of the duties and other regulations of commerce...shall...be based upon an overall assessment of weighted average tariff rates and of customs duties collected...For this purpose, the duties and charges to be taken into consideration shall be the applied rates of duty. It is recognized that for the purpose of the overall assessment of the incidence of other regulations of commerce for which quantification and aggregation are difficult, the examination of individual measures, regulations, products covered and trade flows affected may be required.

3. The "reasonable length of time" referred to in Article XXIV 5(c) should exceed ten years only in exceptional cases.

GATS Article V

1. This Agreement shall not prevent any of its Members from being a party to or entering into an agreement liberalizing trade in services

between or among the parties to such an agreement, provided that such an agreement:

(a). has substantial sectoral coverage[19] and

(b). provides for the absence or elimination of substantially all discrimination, in the sense of Article XVII, between or among the parties, in the sectors covered under subparagraph (a)....

3(a). Where developing countries are parties to an agreement of the type referred to in paragraph 1, flexibility shall be provided for regarding the conditions set out in paragraph 1, in particular to subparagraph (b), in accordance with the level of development of the countries concerned, both overall and in individual sectors and subsectors...

4. Any agreement referred to in paragraph 1 shall be designed to facilitate trade between the parties to the agreement and shall not in respect of any Member outside the agreement raise the overall level of barriers to trade in services within the respective sectors or subsectors compared to the level applicable prior to such an agreement.

Notes

1. Multilateral trade liberalization means nearly all countries reducing barriers on imports from nearly all partners.

2. We have already discussed some of the different incentives for external tariff setting in CUs as compared to FTAs (chapter 4), where we argued that CUs might be inclined to higher tariffs than FTAs. Krugman's analysis concentrates on CUs.

3. In addition, the welfare loss due to trade diversion for a given level of tariffs is greatest when trade is fairly evenly divided between partner and nonpartner countries.

4. Effective RIAs among developing countries (up to 1995) are defined as including: CACM (1960–75; since 1990); Andean Pact (since 1990), MERCOSUR, UEMOA, and SACU. Individual countries affected by their RIA memberships include: Cameroon, Israel, Kenya, Mexico, and Zimbabwe.

5. The interwar period offers further examples. Between the 1920s and the mid-1930s the world trading system switched rapidly from being relatively even-handed to a pattern of regional preferences. First Britain and France introduced colonial preferences. In response, Germany built its own system of preferences, starting with a proposed customs union with Austria in 1931. In 1934 the United States responded with the Reciprocal Trade Agreements Act.

6. Frankel's model is not at all robust, but it does demonstrate formally the interaction between RIAs.

7. Levy (1995) shows theoretically how acquiring fringes of FTA partners could weaken EU and U.S. interest in mutual negotiations.

8. Oye (1992) argues that the 1930s also fit this description. He argues that regional arrangements, such as U.S. bilateral arrangements, under the Reciprocal Trade

Agreements Act were politically feasible, because they almost guaranteed export expansion in partner markets in return for import liberalization. In this way they started to relax restrictions that were immune to multilateral efforts.

9. The rules of international commerce are embodied in three main agreements: GATT, GATS, and the Agreement on Trade-Related Aspects of Intellectual Property Rights. They are administered by the WTO, two of whose major tools are the Trade Policy Review Mechanism and the Understanding on Dispute Settlement. The WTO has 132 members; the major nonmember economies, all of which are seeking accession, are China, Russia, Saudi Arabia, and Taiwan (China); the other major group of current candidates are the countries of Eastern Europe and Central Asia.

10. For example, if a country is harmed by another's breaking into its export markets, there is "properly" no redress under the GATT.

11. For example, in reviewing the treaty, the GATT executive secretary expressed the view, with which he thought there was no disagreement, that the incidence of the common tariff was higher than that of the rates actually applied by the member states at the time of entry into force of the Treaty of Rome (GATT Document C/M/8 p.6; cited in GATT 1994, p. 750).

12. Under GATT procedure, finding a party in violation of its obligations required unanimity. This is not true of WTO.

13. Within the GATT there was a feeling that the article had influenced the structure of U.S.-Canadian and U.S.-Israeli agreements (private communication). We can also identify cases where WTO rules, or their equivalent, have prevented RIAs. For example, in 1932 Britain and

the United States refused to waive their MFN rights, preventing the implementation of the Ouchy Convention, a forerunner of Benelux (Viner 1950). Similarly, negotiators of the draft Multilateral Agreement on Investment found no way of preventing some concessions on services among member from also applying to nonmembers via the GATS MFN clause. Hence, they held back such concessions. GATS Article V permits regional arrangements, but the Multilateral Agreement on Investment was far too narrowly defined to qualify.

14. Together these requirements seem to impose no discipline on the sectors that are excluded from the RIA, although they may still be covered by the members' GATS obligations.

15. The Decision on Differential and More Favorable Treatment, Reciprocity and Fuller Participation of Developing Countries (1979).

16. There is also an unresolved dispute about whether Article XXIV can be applied to an arrangement notified under the Enabling Clause, as the United States demands for MERCOSUR.

17. The EU has explicitly decided that it will not propose any changes to Articles XXIV and V in the next round of trade talks.

18. The United States and its partners still use the WTO dispute settlement, but in recent years there has been no WTO dispute between the EU and any country with which it has a formal RIA.

19. This condition is understood in terms of number of sectors, volume of trade affected, and modes of supply. In order to meet this condition, agreements should not provide for the *a priori* exclusion of any mode of supply.

CHAPTER 6

Conclusion: Tell Me the Truth about Trade Blocs

Trade blocs are political...

URING THE 1990S TRADE BLOCS PROLIFERATED. BY 1999 MORE regional agreements had been notified to the WTO than it had countries as members. Evidently, there were powerful forces driving this process. These forces were political: trade blocs have economic effects, but that is not why they are established. The main political objective has probably been enhanced security. International trade reduces the risks of military conflict between countries and so there might appear to be a reasonable case for preferentially promoting trade relations between neighbors. Unfortunately, whereas international trade is normally mutually beneficial, preferentially induced trade can sometimes create powerful transfers so that one partner gains at the expense of another. There are numerous historical examples of such redistributions causing conflict because they are seen as unfair. Hence, even when the objective of a regional arrangement is purely political, the economic consequences need to be understood.

Another motivation has been to enhance bargaining power. OPEC demonstrated that it was possible under some conditions to improve the terms of trade by collective action. The scope for OPEC-type trade agreements proved very limited. However, small developing countries may still find that by negotiating collectively with industrial countries on trade issues they would gain, not by increasing their power, but by enhancing their ability to get noticed in bargaining rounds, enabling them to conclude more reciprocal deals.

Regional cooperation on trade issues may help countries to cooperate on other issues. Small neighboring countries have plenty of scope for cooperation. Some infrastructure, such as power, telecoms, and railways, may be better provided regionally than nationally. If the tax treatment of multinationals is harmonized, countries can increase their bargaining power and avoid a race to the bottom. Thus, even if regional cooperation starts with trade issues, it should not stop there. The main benefit from cooperation on trade issues may be the development of a habit of trust and cooperation between neighboring governments that can then be extended to issues on which there is more scope for mutual gain.

Many developing and transition economies are in the process of reforming their economic policies and their governance systems. Regional cooperation has sometimes proved useful as a commitment mechanism, locking in the change. The most spectacular examples of this have probably been the North-South cooperation arrangements: Mexico gaining credibility through NAFTA, Eastern Europe through accession agreements with the EU, and North Africa through association agreements with the EU. Some South-South agreements have also acted as commitment mechanisms, notably MERCOSUR.

Security, bargaining power, cooperation, and lock-in are probably the main political motors for regional integration. Sometimes these motives receive a veneer of economic rationalization. Frequently there is an appeal to the benefits flowing from scale economies. Such "soundbites" of economic analysis are not usually wrong, but they are so incomplete and lopsided as to be seriously misleading: weapons casually hurled by advocates who have already decided their position, rather than serious attempts to understand the economic consequences of choices.

The politically feasible alternative to a costly trade bloc is probably a better-designed bloc...

IN THIS REPORT WE HAVE TREATED THE POLITICAL FORCES FOR the creation of regional arrangements as largely unstoppable and have focused on choices of design. For example, only if regional schemes adopt common external tariffs, such as in the EU, can they bargain collectively in world trade rounds. Yet a common tariff precludes unilateral liberalization, and also prevents individual developing countries from joining their appropriate product-based groupings in global negotiations. Thus, schemes that do not adopt a common external tariff probably have a lower opportunity cost in terms of other trade policy options. It is therefore more reasonable to treat the effects of such schemes as being additional to whatever unilateral and global liberalization might be underway. This has been our approach in analyzing the effects of trade blocs.

So how does a trade bloc affect people, especially the poorest?

I N ORDER TO MAKE SENSE OF DESIGN CHOICES, THE BASIC economic effects of trade blocs need to be understood. The overall policy message is that the effects are very sensitive to the choices of design. It matters enormously who else is in the bloc and how preferences are implemented. We distinguish between two broad types of effect: the first is competition and scale, and the second is trade and location.

Competition and Scale Effects

The simple "soundbite" image of the benefits of a trade bloc is perhaps the scale benefits of having a single big factory serving the regional market. This will almost never be a good idea. Such a factory would be a protected monopoly, and such monopolies are usually inefficient and exploitative. Competition is a vital discipline on private behavior, yet there is obviously a tradeoff between the number of competitors in a market and the average size of factory. More competition means smaller factories, and so within any given market there is a tradeoff between competition and scale. Regional integration enlarges the market and so enables both more competition and a larger average scale. Instead of having two national markets, each with three firms producing 100 units, there can be four firms in the regional market, each of which produces 150 units. Both the increase in competition and the increase in scale will lower prices, as we have shown happened in MERCOSUR; so regional integration will have been beneficial, but in order to reap these gains, two of the six firms will have closed. Hence, in order for regional integration to secure the gains of competition and scale, the least efficient firms must be allowed to exit. A successful regional integration is an omelet that cannot be made without breaking eggs. Furthermore, removing tariffs is likely to be insufficient to achieve these gains that depend upon national markets becoming integrated into a single regional market. This will require many other supporting policies of "deep integration" to harmonize product standards and ensure that all firms have real penetration in all the nations within the region.

A trade bloc that succeeds in reaping these competition and scale effects will not only lower the prices of manufactures produced within the region. As a result, importers will be forced to lower their prices so the bloc will improve its terms of trade. If developing countries want to use trade blocs to improve their terms of trade, the most pertinent model is not OPEC but MERCOSUR. The policy instrument is thus not a collective increase in trade taxes, but a collective increase in competition.

Trade and Location Effects

Competition and scale effects accrue to the region as a whole, but trade and location effects are predominantly about transfers between one part of the region and another. The key trade effect is that money, which prior to the trade bloc accrued to the government as tariff revenue, will now accrue to firms in the partner country. The government loses tariff revenue and the country as a whole loses income. This effect is known as trade diversion. We have looked to see how substantial this effect is in seven recent regional arrangements by modeling the effect on trade between the countries in the bloc and the rest of the world. In four of the seven there was no problem, but in three the problem was large enough to be visible. Hence, diversion is neither so common as to be general, nor so unusual as to be dismissable. The analysis has to be done bloc by bloc. In some circumstances the loss of revenue will be serious, notably where tariffs are high and tariff revenue is a substantial share of total government revenue. For example, in a small, poor country such as Burkina Faso, regional integration will involve a large diversion from government revenue to manufacturing firms in Côte d'Ivoire and Senegal. A price that Burkina Faso might have to pay for the political drive to regionalism might thus be fewer children in primary education. Recent research suggests that there may be a further hidden cost to diversion. One by-product of trade is knowledge: firms learn from their trading partners. Evidence shows that trade has more knowledge benefits the larger is the stock of knowledge of the trading partner, with the stock of knowledge measured by the accumulated investment in research and development. Hence, if a poor Southern country diverts its trade from a Northern country with a large knowledge stock, to another Southern country with a much smaller knowledge stock, it will reduce its learning. Since within a South-South trade bloc it is the poorest countries that experience the most diversion, they are the ones liable to suffer the largest reduction in knowledge transfer.

The formation of a trade bloc will cause economic activities to shift location. Potentially, this can create convergence or divergence between the members of the bloc. One contribution of this report has been the discovery that the conventional forces of comparative advantage have a disturbing implication for South-South trade blocs. We show that comparative advantage produces convergence in North-North blocs, but divergence in South-South blocs. We show that this is not just theory. In the EU the poorer Northern countries, such as Ireland, Portugal, and Spain, have caught up with the richer countries: there are dramatic signs of convergence. By contrast, in CACM and the Economic Community of West Africa there are symptoms of divergence: the richer Southern countries have substantially gained market share at the expense of the poorer. Comparative advantage works in this way in these trade blocs by advantaging the middle-income countries. A North-North bloc discriminates against the South and so helps those countries within the bloc that are the closest competitors with the South, namely the lowest-income countries in the bloc. A South-South bloc discriminates against the North and so helps those countries within the bloc that are the closest competitors with the North, namely the highest-income countries in the bloc. Thus, the same force produces convergence in Northern blocs and divergence in Southern blocs.

A further force for divergence within Southern blocs is industrial agglomeration. Firms within an industry gain from clustering together, and when freed from trade barriers will choose to do so. Trade blocs will thus always increase agglomeration within each industry: if they fail to do so it is because they have failed to remove the real barriers to trade. Such forces may or may not cause overall industrial agglomeration. For example, in the United States, although each industry is highly agglomerated, there is little overall industrial agglomeration because different industries cluster in different cities. The key issue is whether the big gains from agglomeration are specific to each industry or accrue to industry in general. These processes have not yet been very thoroughly researched empirically, but what seems probable is that at an early stage of industrialization the main benefits of clustering accrue for industry as a whole—for example, the provision of good infrastructure—whereas at an advanced stage the main benefits are industry-specific—for example, a skilled work force. Unfortunately, as with the forces of comparative advantage, this will also tend to produce convergence within Northern blocs and divergence within Southern blocs. These forces for divergence within Southern trade blocs have evident and serious implications for poverty. They may also make the blocs politically unviable and even become a cause of conflict.

I'm the minister of trade. What bloc design should I choose?

TAKING THE POLITICAL IMPETUS FOR THE FORMATION OF trade blocs as a given, it is evident that the poorest countries may find membership of the conventional South-South blocs quite problematic. While the soundbite regional economics of scale economies might seem to offer most to the poorest, smallest economies, a more serious analysis reveals much scope for loss: revenue diversion, reduced knowledge transfer, and divergence from richer partners. We now review some of the design choices that can determine whether a trade bloc is economically advantageous to all of its members, or is liable to be a source of contention.

Which countries should I take as partners?

TABLE 4.1 SUMMARIZES OUR ASSESSMENT OF PARTNER suitability. For example, a Central European transition economy may look to association with the EU primarily for the political benefits of security and policy lock-in. These political benefits are likely to be so large that the country would probably want to join the trade bloc even if the economic effects were on balance highly negative. In fact, they are likely to be positive. There will probably be some losses from revenue diversion, but the scale and competition, and trade and location effects are likely to be positive. Thus, the political impetus also happens to make economic sense. A trade bloc between two large, middle-income countries can also have very substantial political benefits. Regional security may be enhanced, there may be policy lock-in, the increased trust may facilitate other types of regional cooperation, and negotiating power may increase. The economics are less clear. The increased competition is likely to improve the terms of trade, and this can be a large benefit. If manufacturing is already well established, although there will be powerful and beneficial agglomeration effects within each industry, the bloc may avoid significant overall industrial agglomeration. Offsetting this, there may be some revenue diversion. Thus, the strong political impetus may not deliver commensurate economic benefits, but there is perhaps little danger of large net costs.

The most problematic blocs are evidently those between two small, poor countries, one of which is significantly poorer than the other. There may still be some political gains: the bloc may find it easier to get noticed than the countries individually, and if the experience of trade cooperation builds up trust, it may facilitate cooperation on other issues. However, there may also be political costs as the unintended economic transfers generate frictions. The economic effects look worrying: as discussed above, the poorer country stands to lose through several distinct processes. What else might such poor countries do? One option is for a South-South bloc to negotiate an associate agreement with a Northern bloc. Such a negotiating opportunity is currently available from the EU through the new Lomé agreement, and might also become available from the United States. Politically, membership of a North-South bloc may bring benefits of policy lock-in, as in Central Europe. Economically, it offers enhanced knowledge gains, and should at least mitigate the problem of divergence within the Southern bloc. While the forces of industrial agglomeration would still favor the more developed Southern partner, the forces of comparative advantage would favor the poorest most. Hence, small, poor countries should probably aim to rechannel the political impetus for trade blocs from expanding South-South blocs into South-North blocs. The less-poor members of South-South blocs might also benefit from such a change of strategy. Although they would lose protection in the tiny markets of the poorest countries, they would be the most likely beneficiaries of investment in industries exporting to the new Northern market.

How many blocs should I join?

MORE IS FINE AS LONG AS THEY ARE NOT INCOMPATIBLE, although the resources spent in negotiating and administering them may be better used on other issues. At present some countries have signed multiple agreements that are not legally compatible. This is not merely bad law, it gives rise to investor uncertainty: it is simply unclear which tariffs will actually end up being applied. And even when compatible, a proliferation of agreements may leave investors confused. The existence of incompatible agreements is a classic example of political dreams colliding with practical decisions. In such cases the political impetus to regional agreements needs to be rechanneled.

How much preference should I give?

BIG PREFERENCES CAUSE INDUSTRY TO AGGLOMERATE IN A single location within a South-South trade bloc. This implies strong transfers within the bloc with the poorer members losing out. It is therefore in the interest of the poorer members of a South-South bloc to set their external tariff at a moderate level, and if the bloc has a common tariff, to insist that it be fairly low. Another reason for low external tariffs is that big preferences increase revenue diversion. Also, since protection in poorer members is typically higher than in richer ones, the poorer ones will lose more from opening up to the rich ones than they gain from free access to them. This can be resolved by a reduction in the poor member's external tariff.

Should I press for a common external tariff?

COMMON EXTERNAL TARIFFS HAVE ONE BIG ADVANTAGE: THEY avoid the need for "rules of origin," the enforcement of which creates a large amount of bureaucracy and scope for fraud. However, they also have serious disadvantages. Neighboring countries differ as to their need for tariff revenue, and hence as to the height of tariff that is appropriate. They also differ in their chosen pace of trade liberalization and in their preferences and opportunities for tariff bargaining. Finally, the common pool of revenue has to be divided on some basis, and this may strain political cooperation. In practice, governments usually opt out of a common external tariff through exemptions, even if they sign up in principle.

How deep should I take liberalization?

THE BIG GAINS FROM TRADE BLOCS COME FROM INTEGRATING markets. Removing tariffs but leaving other impediments will inflict all the costs of revenue diversion without any of the compensating benefits of competition and scale. Thus deeper is better. Potentially, agreements can preclude the use of antidumping suits, which is part of the agreement between members of the EU. Since the EU has already extended this benefit to Iceland, there would seem to be in principle no obstacle to its being included in prospective South-North blocs involving the EU. Agreements can also cover border procedures where there is often large scope for illicit protection that undermines the bloc. Finally, as in the EU, they can cover product standards. Rather than agree on common standards, which is slow and may be costly for the poorer members, the most practical step may be mutual recognition: If a product can be sold in one country, it can be sold anywhere in the bloc.

How wide should I let negotiations range?

THE FOCUS OF SOUTHERN TRADE BLOCS IS PRIMARILY ON trade in manufactures. However, many of the big gains to liberalizing trade are to be found in services. Services are often less exposed to competition, and a high-cost service sector can handicap all the other sectors of the economy for which it supplies inputs. It is also important to extend cooperation beyond trade. For example, in South-South blocs that fail to harmonize the taxation of foreign investment, the creation of the trade bloc weakens the bargaining power of each government relative to the investor. The investor can now serve the entire regional market by locating in that country that offers the lowest taxation, and so the trade bloc encourages a tax race to the bottom.

I went to Seattle. How can I use the WTO more effectively?

FINALLY, THE REPORT HAS CONSIDERED TRADE BLOCS IN THE context of the WTO. Developing countries have much to gain from continued multilateral nonpreferential liberalization as enforced by the MFN clause. MFN strengthens the weak by limiting the power of the strong to cut deals with each other that exclude the weak. The biggest exception to MFN that the GATT and WTO have permitted has been the EU, which has fully liberalized trade among its members without extending the same opportunities to other nations.

Developing countries have an interest in protecting the MFN principle from further erosion, but they also have an interest in gaining access to the trade blocs that the North has already constructed. The strategy of imitating the North by constructing South-South blocs is unlikely to be beneficial for the poorest. South-South blocs cannot do for the South what North-North blocs did for the North. This is not because of a lack of political will, it is because the same economic forces will produce radically different outcomes. South-South blocs offer little to the poorest countries and may even harm them.

The poor need secure access to the North, and they can get this in only two ways: through a successful WTO, or through association agreements with the EU, Japan, or the United States. These are, in fact, the two different uses of the term "open regionalism": concerted multilateralism, and open access to membership of the Northern clubs. Fortunately, these are not alternatives. The poor can support the WTO against the menace of Northern protectionist lobbies at the same time that they pressure for the right of access to the clubs. Since this report is about trade blocs, we have focused upon the latter. We have proposed that the WTO modify its rules concerning trade blocs to create a presumptive right of association. Analogous to the MFN clause, if association is granted to one country, there should be a presumption that similar terms should be available to others. If Iceland is offered reciprocal freedom from antidumping suits by the EU, then the same option should be available to Ghana. Naturally, association is complex, and so, in practice, each accession must be negotiated. But the poor should not be denied the association rights already conferred by both the United States and the EU on several middle-income countries. The voice of the poor is not loud in global trade forums and is easily hijacked by Northern special interests. We have proposed a package-negotiating offer by the South to the North concerning the WTO rules governing trade blocs. The South would offer to extend the existing rules concerning North-North trade blocs to South-South blocs. Although this is a concession, it would strengthen the MFN principle, which is very much in the interests of the South. In return, the South would demand an open access rule, in which the right to equal treatment of applications for association in all trade blocs would be enshrined.

Bibliography

Abouyoub, Hasan. 1998. Personal communication at the World Bank conference on "Regionalism and Development." Geneva (May).

Adams, Charles. 1993. *For Good and Evil: The Impact of Taxes on the Course of Civilization.* Lanham, Maryland: Madison Books.

Ades, Alberto F. and Edward L. Glaeser. 1995. "Trade and Circuses: Explaining Urban Giants." *Quarterly Journal of Economics* 110(February): 195–227.

Andriamananjara, Soamiely, and Maurice Schiff. Forthcoming. "Regional Groupings among Microstates." *Review of International Economics.*

Anwar, Dewi F. 1994. *Indonesia in ASEAN: Foreign Policy and Regionalism.* New York: St. Martin's Press.

Bagwell, Kyle, and R.W. Staiger. 1998. "Will Preferential Agreements Undermine the Multilateral Trading System?" *Economic Journal* 108(July): 1162–82.

Baldwin, Richard E. 1989. "The Growth Effects of 1992." *Economic Policy* 9: 247–81.

_____. 1995. "A Domino Theory of Regionalism." In Richard E. Baldwin, P. Haaparanta, and J. Kiander, eds. *Expanding Membership in the European Union,* Cambridge, United Kingdom: Cambridge University Press.

Baldwin, Richard E., and Anthony Venables. 1997. "International Economic Integration." In G. Grossman and K. Rogoff, eds., *Handbook of International Economics,* volume 3. Amsterdam: North Holland.

Baldwin, Richard E., R. Forslid, and J. Haaland. 1996. "Investment Creation and Investment Diversion: A Simulation Study of the EU's Single Market Programme." *World Economy* 19(6): 635–59.

Barry, Frank, and John Bradley. 1997. "FDI and Trade: The Irish Host-Country Experience." *Economic Journal* 107(November): 1798–1811.

Basevi, G., F. Delbono, and M. Mariotti. 1995. "Bargaining with a Composite Player: An Application to the Uruguay Round of GATT Negotiations." *Journal of International Comparative Economics* 3:161–74.

Bayoumi, Tamim, and Barry Eichengreen. 1997. "Is Regionalism Simply a Diversion: Evidence from the Evolution of the EC and EFTA." In T. Ito and Anne O. Krueger, eds., *Regionalism Versus Multilateral Trade Arrangements*. National Bureau of Economic Research. East Asia Seminar on Economics, vol. 6, Chicago: University of Chicago Press.

Ben-David, Dan. 1993. "Equalizing Exchange: Trade Liberalization and Income Convergence." *Quarterly Journal of Economics* 108(3): 653–79.

Bergsten, C. Fred. 1996. "Globalizing Free Trade." In Jeffrey J. Schott, ed. The World Trading System: Challenges Ahead. Washington, D.C.: Institute for International Economics.

_____. 1997. "APEC in 1997: Prospects and Possible Strategies." Special report 9, pp. 3–17. Washington, D.C. : Institute for International Economics.

Bhagwati, Jagdish. 1993. "Regionalism and Multilateralism: An Overview." In Jaime de Melo and A. Panagariya, eds., *New Dimensions in Regional Integration*. London: Centre for Economic Policy Research.

Bhagwati, Jagdish, and Arvind Panagariya. 1996. "Preferential Trading Areas and Multilateralism—Strangers, Friends, or Foes?" In J. Bhagwati and A. Panagariya, eds., *The Economics of Preferential Trade Agreements*. Washington, D.C.: American Enterprise Institute Press.

Bilal, Sanousi. 1998. "Why Regionalism May Increase the Demand for Trade Protection." *Journal of Economic Integration* 13(1): 30–61.

Blomstrom, Magnus, and Ari Kokko. 1997a. "Regional Integration and Foreign Direct Investment: A Conceptual Framework and Three Cases." Policy Research Working Paper no. 1750. World Bank, Washington, D.C.

_____. 1997b. "How Foreign Investment Affects Host Countries." Policy Research Working Paper no. 1745. World Bank, Washington, D.C.

Bond, Eric W., and Constantinos Syropoulos. 1996a. "The Size of Trading Blocs: Market Power and World Welfare Effects." *Journal of International Economics* 40(May): 411–37.

_____. 1996b. "Trading Blocs and the Sustainability of Inter-regional Cooperation." In M. Canzoneri, W. Ethier, and V. Grilli, eds., *The New Transatlantic Economy*, Cambridge, United Kingdom: Cambridge University Press.

Bouzas, Roberto. 1997. "MERCOSUR's Economic Agenda: Short and Medium-term Policy Challenges." Integration and Trade 10:64–5.

Catinat, M., and A. Italianer. 1998. "Completing the Internal Market: Primary Microeconomic Effects and their Implementation in Macroeconometric Models." Commission of the European Communities.

Chang, Won, and Maurice Schiff. 1999. "Regional Integration and the Price Effects of Contestability." World Bank Development Economics Research Group, International Trade Unit, Washington, D.C. Processed.

Chang, Won, and L. Alan Winters. 1999. "How Regional Blocs Affect Excluded Countries: The Price

Effects of MERCOSUR." Discussion Paper Series no. 2179. Centre for Economic Policy Research, London.

Coe, David T., and Elhanan Helpman. 1995. "International R&D Spillovers." *European Economic Review* 39(5): 859–87.

Coe, David T., Elhanan Helpman, and Alexander W. Hoffmaister. 1997. "North-South R&D Spillovers." *Economic Journal* 107: 134–49.

Collier, Paul, and J.W. Gunning. 1995. "Trade Policy and Regional Integration: Implications for the Relations between Europe and Africa." *World Economy* 18:387–410.

Commission of the European Communities. 1995. "Proposal for a Decision of the Council and the Commission on the Conclusion of a Euro-Mediterranean Agreement Establishing an Association between the European Communities and Their Member States and the Republic of Tunisia." COM(95)235 final (May 31).

De la Torre, Augusto, and M. Kelley. 1992. *Regional Trade Arrangements*. Washington D.C.: International Monetary Fund.

De Rosa, Dean A. 1995. "Regional Trading Arrangements among Developing Countries: The ASEAN Example." Research Report no. 103. International Food Policy Research Institute, Washington D.C.

Dickens, William, and Lawrence Katz. 1987. "Inter-Industry Wage Differences and Industry Characteristics." In Kevin Lang and Jonathan Leonard, eds., *Unemployment and the Structure of Labor Markets*. New York: Blackwell.

Dixit, Avinash. 1988. "Antidumping and Countervailing Duties under Oligopoly." *European Economic Review* 32:55–68.

Djankov, Simeon, and Bernard Hoekman. 1997. "Effective Protection and Investment Incentives in Egypt and Jordan: Implications of Free Trade with Europe." *World Development* 25:281–91.

_____. 1998. "Avenues of Technology Transfer: Foreign Investment and Productivity Change in the Czech Republic." Working Paper 16/98. Fondazione Eni Enrico Mattei Note di Lavoro.

Engel, Charles, and John H. Rogers. 1996. "How Wide is the Border?" *American Economic Review* 86(5): 1112–25.

Feenstra, Robert, and Gordon Hanson. 1997. "Foreign Direct Investment and Relative Wages: Evidence from Mexico's Maquiladoras." *Journal of International Economics* 42: 371–93.

Fernandez, Raquel, and Jonathan Portes. 1998. "Returns to Regionalism: An Analysis on Nontraditional Gains from Regional Trade Agreements." *World Bank Economic Review* 12(2):197–220.

Finger, J. Michael. 1993. *Antidumping: How it Works and Who Gets Hurt*. Ann Arbor, Michigan: University of Michigan Press.

Flores, R. 1997. "The Gains from MERCOSUL: A General Equilibrium, Imperfect Competition Evaluation." *Journal of Policy Modeling* 19: 1–18.

Foroutan, Faezeh. 1993. "Regional Integration in Sub-Saharan Africa: Past Experience and Future Prospects." In Jaime de Melo and Arvind

Panagariya, eds., *New Dimensions in Regional Integration*. London: Center for Economic Policy Research.

_____. 1996. "Turkey, 1976–85: Foreign Trade, Industrial Productivity, and Competition." In Mark J. Roberts and James R. Tybout, eds., *Industrial Evolution in Developing Countries: Micro Patters of Turnover, Productivity, and Market Structure*. Oxford, United Kingdom: Oxford University Press.

_____. 1998. "Does Membership of a Regional Preferential Trade Arrangement Make a Country More or Less Protectionist?" *The World Economy* 21: 305–36.

Francois, Joseph. 1997. "External Bindings and the Credibility of Reform." In A. Galal and B. Hoekman, eds., *Regional Partners in Global Markets*. London: Center for Economic Policy Research.

Francois, J., and C. Shiells. 1994. *Modeling Trade Policy: Applied General Equilibrium Assessments of North American Free Trade*. Cambridge, United Kingdom: Cambridge University Press.

Frankel, Jeffrey. 1997. *Regional Trading Blocs in the World Economic System*. Washington, D.C.: Institute for International Economics.

Fujita, Masahisa, Paul Krugman, and Anthony Venables. 1999. *The Spatial Economy: Cities, Regions, and International Trade*. Cambridge, Massachusetts: MIT Press.

Fukase, Emiko, and L. Alan Winters. 1999. "Possible Dynamic Benefits of ASEAN/AFTA Accession for the New Member Countries." World Bank, Washington, D.C. Processed.

Fukase, Emiko, and William Martin. 1999. "Evaluating the Implications of Cambodia's Accession to the ASEAN Free Trade Area: A General Equilibrium Model (CGE) Approach." World Bank, Washington, D.C. Processed.

Gatsios, Konstantine, and Larry Karp. 1991. "Delegation Games in Customs Unions." *Review of Economic Studies* 58(2): 391–97.

_____. 1995. "Delegation in a General Equilibrium Model of Customs Unions." *European Economic Review* 39(2): 319–33.

GATT (General Agreement on Tariffs and Trade). 1994. "Report on Regional Integration." Secretariat, Geneva.

Gordon, H., S. Rimmer, and S. Arrowsmith. 1998. "The Economic Impact of the EU Regime on Public Procurement." *World Economy* 21:159–88.

Grossman, G., and E. Helpman. 1994. "Protection for Sale." *American Economic Review* 84(4): 833–50.

_____. 1995. "The Politics of Free-Trade Agreements." *American Economic Review* 85(4): 667–90.

Gupta, Anju, and Maurice Schiff. 1997. "Outsiders and Regional Trade Agreements among Small Countries: The Case of Regional Markets." Policy Research Working Paper no. 1847. World Bank, Washington, D.C.

Haddad, Mona. 1993. "The Effect of Trade Liberalization on Multi-factor Productivity: The Case of Morocco." Discussion Paper Series no.4, World Bank, Washington, D.C.

Haddad, Mona, and Ann Harrison. 1993. "Are There Positive Spillovers from Direct Foreign Investment? Evidence from Panel Data for Morocco." *Journal of Development Economics* 42: 51–74.

Haddad, Mona, Jaime de Melo, and Brendan Horton. 1996. "Morocco, 1984–89: Trade Liberalization, Exports and Industrial Performance." In Mark J. Roberts, and James R. Tybout, eds., *Industrial Evolution in Developing Countries: Micro Patters of Turnover, Productivity, and Market Structure*. Oxford, United Kingdom: Oxford University Press.

Hansen, Lyle M. 1969. "The Economy of Burundi." Report AE–1a. International Bank for Reconstruction and Development, Washington, D.C.

Hanson, Gordon. 1996. "Economic Integration, Intraindustry Trade and Frontier Regions." *European Economic Review* 40: 941–49.

Harrison, Ann. 1994. "Productivity, Imperfect Competition, and Trade Reform." *Journal of International Economics* 36: 53–73.

_____. 1996. "Openness and Growth: A Time-Series, Cross-Country Analysis for Developing Countries." *Journal of Development Economics* 48(2): 419–47.

Harrison, Glenn, Thomas Rutherford, and David Tarr. 1994. "Product Standards, Imperfect Competition and the Completion of the Market in the EC." Policy Research Working Paper no. 1293. World Bank, Washington, D.C.

Hathaway, Dale E., and Merlinda D. Ingco. 1996. "Agricultural Liberalization and the Uruguay Round." In William Martin and L. Alan Winters, eds., *The Uruguay Round and the Developing Countries*. Cambridge, United Kingdom: Cambridge University Press.

Helliwell, J. 1997. "How Much Do National Borders Matter?" Series on Integrating National Economies. The Brookings Institution, Washington, D.C.

Herin, Jan. 1986. "Rules of Origin and Differences between Tariff Levels in EFTA and the EC." Occasional Paper no. 13. European Free Trade Association, Secretariat, Geneva.

Hillman, Arye. 1989. "The Political Economy of Protection." *Fundamentals of Pure and Applied Economics*. Switzerland, London, New York: Harmead Academic.

Hirschman, Albert O. 1958. *The Strategy of Economic Development*. New Haven, Connecticut: Yale University Press.

_____. 1981. *Essays in Trespassing: Economics to Politics and Beyond*. Cambridge, United Kingdom: Cambridge University Press.

Hoekman, Bernard. 1998. "Preferential Trade Agreements." In R. Lawrence, ed., *Brookings Trade Forum 1998*. Washington, D.C.: The Brookings Institution.

_____. 1999. "Rents, Red Tape, and Regionalism: Economic Effects of Deeper Integration." In B. Hoekman, and J. Zarrouk, eds., *Catching up with the Competition: Trade Opportunities and Challenges for Arab Countries*. Ann Arbor, Michigan: University of Michigan Press.

Hoekman, Bernard, and Michael Leidy. 1993. "Holes and Loopholes in Regional Integration Agreements." In Kym Anderson and Richard Blackhurst, eds., *Regional Integration.* London: Harvester-Wheatsheaf.

Hoekman, Bernard, and Carlos Primo Braga. 1997. "Protection and Trade in Services: A Survey." *Open Economies Review* 8: 285–308.

Hoekman, Bernard, and Denise Konan. 1999. "Deep Integration, Nondiscrimination, and Euro-Mediterranean Free Trade." Discussion Paper no. 2095. Centre for Economic Policy Research, London.

Hoekman, Bernard, and Michel Kostecki. 1995. "The Political Economy of the World Trading System: From GATT to WTO." Oxford and New York: Oxford University Press.

Hoekman, Bernard, and Petros C. Mavroidis, eds. 1997. *Law and Policy in Public Purchasing: The WTO Agreement on Government Procurement.* Ann Arbor, Michigan: University of Michigan Press.

Hoekman, Bernard, and Pierre Sauvé. 1994. Regional and Multilateral Liberalization of Trade in Services: Complements or Substitutes?" *Journal of Common Market Studies* 32: 283–317.

Horn, Henrik, Harold Lang, and Stefan Lundgren. 1995. "Managerial Effort Incentives, X-Inefficiency and International Trade." *European Economic Review* 39: 117–38.

Hunter, Linda, James R. Markusen, and Thomas F. Rutherford. 1992. "U.S.–Mexico Free Trade and the North American Auto Industry: Effects on the Spatial Organization of Production of Finished Autos." *World Economy* 15(1): 65–81.

IDB (Inter-American Development Bank). 1998. "Integration and Trade in the Americas." *Periodic Note* (August).

Irwin, Douglas. 1993. "Multilateral and Bilateral Trade Policies in the World Trading System: An Historical Perspective." in Jaime de Melo and Arvind Panagariya, eds., *New Dimensions in Regional Integration.* London: Centre for Economic Policy Research.

_____. 1996. *Against the Tide: An Intellectual History of Free Trade.* Princeton, New Jersey: Princeton University Press.

Islam, Nurul. 1981. Foreign Trade and Economic Controls in Development: The Case of United Pakistan. New Haven and London: Yale University Press.

Jacquemin, A., and Andre Sapir. 1991. "Competition and Imports in the European Market." In L. Alan Winters and Anthony J. Venables, eds., *European Integration: Trade and Industry.* Cambridge, New York, Melbourne: Cambridge University Press.

Kahler, Miles. 1995. *International Institutions and the Political Economy of Integration.* Washington, D.C.: The Brookings Institution.

Kant, Emanuel. 1795. *Perpetual Peace: A Philosophical Essay.* Bristol, United Kingdom: Thoemmes Press.

Kechichian, Joseph. 1985. "The Gulf Cooperation Council: The Search for Security." *Third World Quarterly* 7: 853–81.

Keller, Wolfgang. 1998. "Are International R&D Spillovers Trade-Related? Analyzing Spillovers among Randomly Matched Trade Partners." *European Economic Review* 42(8): 1469–81.

Krishna, Pravin, and Devashish Mitra. 1997. "Trade Liberalization, Market Discipline, and Productivity Growth: New Evidence from India." Brown University, Providence, Rhode Island. Processed.

Krueger, Anne O. 1997. "Free Trade Agreements Versus Customs Union." *Journal of Development Economics* 54: 169–87.

Krugman, Paul. 1991a. "Is Bilateralism Bad?" In E. Helpman and A. Razin, eds., *International Trade and Trade Policy.* Cambridge, Massachusetts: MIT Press.

_____. 1991b. "The Move towards Free Trade Zones." In *Policy Implications of Trade and Currency Zones.* A symposium sponsored by the Federal Reserve Bank of Kansas City, Jackson Hole, Wyoming.

_____. 1993. "Regionalism Versus Multilateralism: Analytical Notes." In Jaime de Melo and Arvind Panagariya, eds., *New Dimensions in Regional Integration.* Cambridge, New York, Melbourne: Cambridge University Press.

Krugman, Paul, and Gordon Hanson. 1993. "Mexico-U.S. Free Trade and the Location of Production." In Peter Garber, ed*., The Mexico-U.S. Free Trade Agreement.* Cambridge, Massachusetts; London: MIT Press.

Lawrence, Robert Z. 1991. "Emerging Regional Arrangements: Building Blocs or Stumbling Blocks?" In O'Brien, ed., *Finance and the International Economy 5: The AMEX Bank.* Review Prize Essays. New York: Oxford University Press.

_____. 1996. *Regionalism, Multilateralism, and Deeper Integration.* Washington, D.C.: The Brookings Institution.

Levinsohn, James. 1993. "Testing the Imports-as-Market-Discipline Hypothesis." *Journal of International Economics* 35: 1–22.

Levy, Philip. 1995. "Free Trade Agreements and Inter-Bloc Tariffs." Yale University, New Haven, Connecticut. Processed.

Madani, Dorsati. 1999. "South-South Regional Integration and Industrial Growth: The Case of the Andean Pact." World Bank, Washington, D.C. Processed.

Magee, Stephen P., and Hak-Loh Lee. 1997. "Tariff Creation and Tariff Diversion in a Customs Union: The Endogenous External Tariff of the EEC 1968–83." *Fondazione Eni Enrico Mattei Note di Lavoro* 38(97).

Marshall, Alfred. 1920. *Principles of Economics.* London: MacMillan.

Mattoo, Aaditya, and Petros Mavroidis. 1995. "The EC-Japan Consensus on Cars: Interactions between Trade and Competition Policy." *World Economy* 18(3): 345–65.

Matusz, Steven J., and David Tarr. 1999. "Adjusting to Trade Policy Reform." Policy Research Working Paper no. 2142. World Bank, Washington, D.C.

McCallum, J. 1995. "National Borders Matter: Canada-US Regional Trade Patterns." *American Economic Review* 85(3): 615–23.

McKibbin, Warwick J. 1994. "Dynamic Adjustment to Regional Integration: Europe 1992 and

139

NAFTA." *Journal of Japanese and International Economics* 8(4): 422–53.

McMillan, John. 1993. "Does Regional Integration Foster Open Trade? Economic Theory and GATT's Article 24." In Kym Anderson and Richard Blackhurst, eds., *Regional Integration and the Global Trading System*. London: Harvester Wheatsheaf.

Melo, Jaime de, Arvind Panagariya, and Dani Rodrik. 1993. "The New Regionalism: A Country Perspective." In Jaime de Melo and Arvind Panagariya, eds., *New Dimensions in Regional Integration*. New York and Melbourne: Cambridge University Press.

Messerlin, Patrick. 1990. "Antidumping Regulations or Pro-Cartel Law? The EC Chemical Cases." *World Economy* 13: 465–92.

_____. 1996. "Competition Policy and Antidumping Reform." Presented at the conference on The World Trading System: Challenges Ahead, June 24–25, Institute for International Economics, Washington D.C.

_____. 1997. "Reforming the Rules of Antidumping Policies." In Horst Siebert, ed., *Towards a New Global Framework for High-Technology Competition*. Institut fur Weltwirtschaft an der Universitat Kiel Symposia and Conference Proceedings. Tubingen: Mohr (Siebeck).

_____. 1998. "Technical Regulations and Industry Standards in the EU." World Bank, Washington, D.C. Processed.

Messerlin, Patrick, and P.K.M. Tharakan. 1999. "The Question of Contingent Protection." *World Economy* 22(9): 1251–70.

Midelfart-Knarvik, H.G., S. Redding Overman, and Anthony J. Venables. 1999. "The Location of Industry in Europe." Centre for Economic Policy Research, London.

Milward, Alan. 1984. *The Reconstruction of Europe, 1945–51*. Berkeley: University of California Press.

_____. 1992. *The European Rescue of the Nation State*. Berkeley: University of California Press.

Milward, Alan, and S.B. Saul. 1973. *The Economic Development of Continental Europe, 1780–1870*. Totowa, New Jersey: Rowman and Littlefield.

Mohieldin, Mahmoud. 1997. "The Egypt-EU Partnership Agreement and Liberalization of Trade in Services." In A. Galal and B. Hoekman, eds., *Regional Partners in Global Markets: Limits and Possibilities of the Euro-Med Agreements*. London: Centre for Economic Policy Research.

Murphy, Craig. 1994. *International Organization and Industrial Change: Global Governance since 1850*. New York: Oxford University Press.

Neven, Damien. 1996. "Regulatory Reform and the Internal Market." Processed.

Nishimuzi, Mieko, and John M. Page. 1982. "Total Factor Productivity Growth, Technological Progress, and Technical Efficiency Change: Dimensions of Productivity Change in Yugoslavia." *Economic Journal* 92: 920–36.

Nogues, Julio J., and Rosalinda Quintanilla. 1993. "Latin America's Integration and the Multilateral Trading System." In Jaime de Melo and Arvind Panagariya, eds., *New Dimensions in Regional*

Integration. London: Centre for Economic Policy Research.

Olarreaga, Marcelo, and Isidro Soloaga. 1998. "Explaining MERCOSUR's Tariff Structure: A Political Economy Approach." *World Bank Economic Review* 12(2): 297–320.

Oye, Kenneth. 1992. *Economic Discrimination and Political Exchange: World Political Economy in the 1930s and 1980s.* Princeton, New Jersey: Princeton University Press.

Page, Sheila. 1996. "Intensity Measures for Regional Groups." Paper prepared for the European Association of Development Research Institutes. Ninth General Conference, Vienna, September.

_____. 1997. "Regions and Developing Countries." Overseas Development Adminstration, London.

Panagariya, Arvind, and Ronald Findlay. 1994. "A Political Economy Analysis of Free Trade Areas and Customs Unions." Policy Research Working Paper no. 1261. World Bank, Washington, D.C.

Pelkmans, Jacques, L. Alan Winters, and Helen Wallace. 1998. *Europe's Domestic Market.* Chatham House Papers Series no. 43. New York and London: Royal Institute of International Affairs.

Pohl, Gerhard, and Piritta Sorsa. 1992. *European Integration and Trade with the Developing World.* Policy and Research Series no. 21. Washington, D.C.: World Bank.

Polachek, Solomon W. 1992. "Conflict and Trade: An Economics Approach to Political Interactions." In Walter Isard and Charles H. Anderton, eds.,

Economics of Arms Reduction and the Peace Process. Amsterdam: North-Holland.

_____. 1997. "Why Democracies Cooperate More and Fight Less: The Relationship between International Trade and Cooperation." *Review of International Economics* 5(1): 295–309.

Pollard, Sidney. 1974. *European Economic Integration, 1815–1970.* London: Thames and Hudson.

Pomfret, Richard. 1997. *The Economics of Regional Trading Arrangements.* New York: Oxford University Press.

Porter, Michael. 1998. *On Competition.* Cambridge, Massachusetts: Harvard Business School Press.

Richardson, Martin. 1994. "Customs Unions and Domestic Taxes." *Canadian Journal of Economics* 27(3): 79–96.

Ricupero, Rubens. 1998. "What Policy Makers Should Know about Regionalism." Keynote Address presented at the World Bank Conference on What Policy Makers Should Know about Regionalism, Geneva, May.

Roberts, Mark, and James Tybout, eds. 1996. *Industrial Evolution in Developing Countries: Micro Patters of Turnover, Productivity, and Market Structure.* Oxford, United Kingdon: Oxford University Press.

Robson, Peter. 1998. *The Economics of International Integration.* London: Routledge.

Rodrik, Dani. 1988. "Imperfect Competition, Scale Economies, and Trade Policy in Developing Countries." In R.E. Baldwin, ed., *Trade Policy Issues and*

Empirical Analysis. Chicago: University of Chicago and National Bureau of Economic Research.

Roy, Jayanta. 1998. "Trade Facilitation: The World Bank Experience." Paper presented at a World Trade Organization Trade Facilitation Symposium, Geneva, Switzerland, March.

Rutherford, Thomas, Elisabet E. Rutström, and David Tarr. 1999. "The Free-Trade Agreement between the European Union and a Representative Arab Mediterranean Country: A Quantitative Assessment." In B. Hoekman and J. Zarrouk, eds., *Catching up with the Competition: Trade Policy Challenges in the Middle East and North Africa.* Ann Arbor, Michigan: University of Michigan Press.

Saggi, Kamal. 1999. "Trade, Foreign Direct Investment, and International Technology Transfer." Southern Methodist University, Dallas, Texas. Processed.

Sapir, Andre. 1993. "The European Community: A Case of Successful Integration? A Comment." In Jaime de Melo and Arvind Panagariya, eds., *New Dimensions in Regional Integration.* London: Centre for Economic Policy Research.

Schiff, Maurice. 1997. "Small Is Beautiful: Preferential Trade Agreements and the Impact of Country Size, Market Share, and Smuggling." *Journal of Economic Integration* 12: 359–87.

_____. 1999. "Will the Real 'Natural Trading Partner' Please Stand Up?" Policy Research Working Paper no. 2161. World Bank, Washington, D.C.

_____. 2000. "Multilateral Trade Liberalization, Political Disintegration, and the Choice of Free Trade Areas Versus Customs Unions." Policy Research Working Paper Series no. 2501. World Bank, Washington, D.C.

Schiff, Maurice, and L. Alan Winters. 1998a. "Regional Integration as Diplomacy." *World Bank Economic Review* 12(2): 271–96.

_____. 1998b. "Regional Integration, Security, and Welfare." In *Regionalism and Development.* Report of the June 1997 European Commission and World Bank Seminar. European Commission Studies Series no. 1. Washington, D.C.: World Bank.

Schmidt, Klaus. 1994. "Managerial Incentives and Product Market Competition." Discussion Paper no. 430. University of Bonn, Bonn.

Schöne, Rainer. 1996. *Alternatives to Antidumping from an Antitrust Perspective.* Ph.D. dissertation, University of St. Gallen. St. Gallen, Switzerland.

Smith, Alasdair, and Anthony Venables. 1988. "Completing the Internal Market in the European Community: Some Industry Simulations." *European Economic Review* 32(7): 1501–25.

Soloaga, Isidro, and L. Alan Winters. 1999a. "How Has Regionalism in the 1990s Affected Trade?" Policy Research Working Paper Series no. 2156. World Bank, Washington, D.C.

_____. 1999b. "Regionalism in the Nineties: What Effect on Trade?" Discussion Paper Series no. 2183. Center for Economic Policy Research. Cambridge, Massachusetts.

Srinivasan, T.N. 1998. "Regionalism and the WTO: Is Nondiscrimination Passé?" In Anne O. Krueger, ed., *The WTO as an International Organization.* Chicago: University of Chicago Press.

Staiger, Robert, and Frank Wolak. 1989. "Strategic Use of Antidumping to Enforce Tacit International Collusion." Working Paper no. 3016. National Bureau of Economic Research. Cambridge, Massachusetts.

Staples, Brian. 1998. "Trade Facilitation." World Bank, Washington, D.C. Processed. Available on http://www.worldbank.org/wbiep/trade/.

Summers, L. 1991. "Regionalism and the World Trading System." In *Policy Implications of Trade and Currency Zones*. A symposium sponsored by the Federal Reserve Bank of Kansas City, Jackson Hole, Wyoming.

Talbott, Strobe. 1996. "Democracy and the National Interest." *Foreign Affairs* 75: 47–63.

Tavares, Jose, and Luis Tineo. 1998. "Harmonization of Competition Policies among MERCOSUR Countries." *Antitrust-Bulletin* 43(1): 45–70.

Tsoukalis, Loukas. 1993. *The New European Economy: The Politics and Economics of European Integration*. Oxford, United Kingdom: Oxford University Press.

Tybout, James. 1999. "Manufacturing Firms in Developing Countries: How Well Do They Do, and Why?" *Journal of Economic Literature* 37(3).

Tybout, James, and M. Daniel Westbrook. 1995. "Trade Liberalization and the Dimensions of Efficiency Change in Mexican Manufacturing Industries." *Journal of International Economics* 39: 53–78.

Tybout, James, Jaime de Melo, and Vittorio Corbo. 1991. "The Effects of Trade Reforms on Scale and Technical Efficiency." *Journal of International Economics* 31: 231–50.

USITC (United States International Trade Commission). 1997. "Study on the Operation and Effects of the NAFTA." Washington, D.C.

Venables, Anthony J. 1999. "Integration Agreements: A Force for Convergence or Divergence?" *Proceedings of World Bank ABCDE Conference*. Policy Research Working Paper Series no. 2260. World Bank, Washington, D.C.

Viner, Jacob. 1950. *The Customs Union Issue*. Washington, D.C.: Carnegie Endowment for International Peace.

Wang, Zhen Kun, and L. Alan Winters. 1998. "Africa's Role in Multilateral Trade Negotiations: Past and Future." *Journal of African Economies* Supplement 1(June): 1–33.

Whalley, John. 1996. "Why Do Countries Seek Regional Trade Agreements?" In J. Frankel, ed., *The Regionalization of the World Economy*. Chicago: Chicago University Press.

Wilmore, Larry. 1976. "Trade Creation, Trade Diversion, and Effective Protection in the Central American Common Market." *Journal of Development Studies* 12: 396–414.

_____. 1978. "The Industrial Economics of Intra-Industry Trade and Specialization." In H. Giersch, ed., *On the Economics of Intra-Industry Trade*. Tubingen, Germany: J.C.B. Mohr.

Winham, G.R. 1986. *International Trade and the Tokyo Round Negotiation*. Princeton, New Jersey: Princeton University Press.

143

Winters, L. Alan. 1992. "The Welfare and Policy Implications of the International Trade Consequences of '1992.'" *American Economic Review* 82(2): 104–108.

_____. 1993. "The European Community: A Case of Successful Integration." Discussion Paper no. 775. Centre for Economic Policy Research, London.

_____. 1994. "The EC and Protection: The Political Economy." *European Economic Review* 38: 596–603.

_____. 1997. "Lebanon's Euro-Mediterranean Agreement: Possible Dynamic Benefits." In W. Shahin and Shehadi K., eds., *Pathways to Integration: Lebanon and the Euro-Mediterranean Partnership.* Bonn: Konrad Adenauer Foundation.

_____. 1999. "Regionalism Versus Multilateralism." In Richard Baldwin, Daniel Cohen, Andre Sapir, and Anthony Venables, eds., *Market Integration, Regionalism and the Global Economy.* Cambridge, United Kingdom: Centre for Economic Policy Research.

Winters, L. Alan, and Won Chang. Forthcoming. "Regional Integration and the Prices of Imports: An Empirical Investigation." *Journal of International Economics.*

Wonnacott, R.I. 1996. "Canadian Trade Policy: The GATT's 1995 Review." *The World Economy* Supplement: 67–80.

Wonnacott, R.I., and Mark Lutz. 1989. "Is there a Case for Free Trade Areas." In Jeffrey Schott, ed., *Free Trade Areas and US Trade Policy.* Washington, D.C.: Institute for International Economics.

World Bank. 1999. *World Development Report 1999.* Washington, D.C.

WTO (World Trade Organization). 1995. "Regionalism and the World Trading System." Geneva: Secretariat.

Yeats, A. 1998. "Does MERCOSUR's Trade Performance Raise Concerns about the Effects of Regional Trade Arrangements?" *The World Bank Economic Review* 12(1): 1–28.